Lesley Rimmer

Occasional paper
Number 6

Families in focus

D1422088

Study Commission on the Family

This occasional paper, like all those in the series, represents the views of the author and not necessarily those of the Study Commission.

The Author

Lesley Rimmer is the Deputy Director of the Family Policy Studies Centre. She was formerly a research officer with the Study Commission on the Family, and a Senior Lecturer in Economics at the Polytechnic of the South Bank.

Acknowledgements

This paper was originally prepared for the Study Commission's working party on the Diversity of Family Patterns. I would like to thank its Chairman, Professor A H Halsey and other members for their help and advice. My thanks also to the Office of Population Censuses and Surveys. I would particularly like to acknowledge the help of Malcolm Wicks, Audrey Brown and Kathleen Kiernan who gave generously of their time and advice and also Lynne Feetham, Chris Rossiter and Jennie Popay.

Responsibility for any errors remains mine.

Published by **Family Policy Studies Centre**
231 Baker Street, London NW1 6XE

Copyright October 1981
Family Policy Studies Centre

Reprinted April 1982, March 1983, December 1984

ISBN 0 907051 08 1

Designed by Ivor Kamlish FSIAD and Associates

Printed in England by
Witley Press Ltd Hunstanton

2

Contents

3

Charts

Tables

All tables and charts with Crown copyright have been reproduced with the permission of the Controller of Her Majesty's Stationery Office.

Introduction

Current discussions about the family — and the controversies they can generate — depend crucially on interpretations about how family patterns and family life are changing. Certainly changes are taking place, but how significant are they? Some changes may signify a departure from traditional patterns and to some represent a threat to the family itself. This paper is **not** intended to give a view about such questions, but rather it seeks to present the best available and most reliable evidence about the family in Britain today.

The purpose of this paper is therefore to paint a statistical picture of various important aspects of family life. It reviews marriage patterns; presents evidence about marital breakdown and remarriage; considers fertility patterns and family size; and presents other evidence about the growth of one parent families, reconstituted families, and old age and the extended family. It concludes by raising some of the policy implications arising from this statistical survey.

Some of the paper's main findings can be briefly stated. Marriage is still 'popular' and, indeed, more young people marry today than was the case 100 years ago. But since the early 1970s marriage rates have declined. More and more marriages are ending in divorce — there were some 138,000 divorces in 1979 and among couples marrying today, some 1 in 4 will end their marriage with a divorce. Divorce affects some 160,000 children every year and we estimate that about 1 in 5 children born today could be affected by the divorce of their parents.

One obvious consequence of divorce is a substantial rise in the number of one parent families. Currently some 920,000 families are headed by just one parent and approximately 1 in 8 children are living today in such families. A far higher proportion will live in one parent families at some stage during the course of their childhood.

At the same time as marriage breakdown is increasing, remarriage is becoming more common. Currently 1 in 3 new marriages involves a remarriage for at least one partner. On the other hand the proportion of divorces involving redivorce for one or other spouse is rising.

7

Patterns of childbearing within marriage have also changed considerably, and an increasing number of families comprise children from more than one marriage.

At the other end of the life cycle there has been a dramatic increase in the number of elderly people. Not only has the total number of elderly people increased by about one third over the last twenty years, but there are growing numbers of the very aged whose needs form an important aspect of contemporary social policy.

These demographic changes have not taken place in isolation. It is outside the scope of the paper to discuss the parallel economic and social changes that have taken place, but it is worth noting the major changes in employment — particularly the increasing paid employment of women — and the development of the welfare state, which have formed an important part of the context of these changes in family patterns. The other major dimensions are the attitudes and values which the changes, and continuities, in family life reflect. A statistical picture such as that presented in the paper cannot hope to do justice to these changes, yet their significance should not be underestimated. Much of the work of the Study Commission is concerned with these issues.

The paper is based almost exclusively on official statistics and surveys, although some smaller, and qualitative studies are cited. While this heavy reliance on official statistics is in some ways a limitation, it is also an important aspect of the paper. Policy makers — both private and public — plan services, benefit systems and programmes on the basis of understandings about the present, and assumptions about the future. Indeed, the whole emphasis on social policy **planning** has made the quality and relevance of the statistical base of particular importance, and official statistics are a central component of this base.

The quality and scope of official statistics on various aspects of family formation have increased dramatically over the last ten years. New social issues generate new needs for information, and it is to be hoped that the valuable contribution that relevant statistics make to 'good' policy making will not be overlooked, especially at a time of rapid social change.

Where possible in the paper the implications of current trends are examined, although this is often a hazardous exercise. The question of how far the current situation is an adequate guide to the future — whether we are hearing 'signal' or 'noise' — is a recurrent theme in the paper.

A serious limitation of much of our knowledge about the family is that we have a snapshot picture at one point in time. For policy making purposes it is often necessary to consider how things change over time, and for this we need longitudinal or time series data. Much **misunderstanding** of social issues arises from using cross sectional data where time series should be used and these and other methodological issues are discussed in Appendix 1.

The paper starts by reviewing the changing structure of the population. In Part 2 evidence is presented about contemporary marriage patterns. Part 3 focusses on fertility and childbearing. Part 4 considers marriage breakdown and divorce. Increased divorce rates have led to a sharp rise in the numbers of one parent families and this trend is analysed in Part 5. Remarriage is reviewed in Part 6, while 'reconstituted' families are considered in Part 7. An important aspect of family life concerns the increasing numbers of the elderly and the 'extended' family is discussed in Part 8. Evidence about changing family patterns is summarised in Part 9 which also discusses briefly the policy implications of this paper's statistical review.

Part 1

The wider context

Our main concerns are family structures and family formation, but these need to be set in the wider context of the growth and components of total population.

Between 1851 and 1901 the population of Great Britain grew by 77%, from 20.8 million to 37 million. Between 1901 and 1951 the rise was 32%, to 49.2 million, and from 1951 to 1971 it was just under 10% to 54.1 million. In 1979 the total population was 54.3 million, and recent estimates suggest that in 1980 the population had reached nearly 54.4 million.[1] It is projected that population will reach 54.6 million by 1985; 55.2 million by 1990; 55.9 million by 1995 and 56.3 million by the year 2000.[2] Between 1980 and 2000, therefore, the population is expected to grow by only 3%, but there will be important changes in the age structure, which are described later. Normally the number of births exceeds the number of deaths, but in 1976, for the first time since the start of civil registrations, the number of deaths exceeded the number of births.[3] This situation continued in 1977 and 1978, but was reversed in 1979.

In contrast to natural increase and with the exception of one or two periods (notably the late '50s and early '60s), international migration represented a relatively small component of population change. Such movements may, however, have more marked effects on births or the age structure, because of the age and family characteristics of migrants. This is equally true and equally important for movements of population within countries.

The Age Structure

From 1850 onwards we have seen an ageing of the population. The total number of elderly people rose from just over 2 million in 1901 to over 9 million in 1971, and to 9.5 million in 1977. The dependency ratio, defined as the sum of the population under school leaving age, plus the population over retirement age, related to the working age population, has not changed dramatically, but the composition of that dependency has changed, with elderly people becoming more, and children less, numerically significant. In the last 20 years the number of men and women over 65 has risen by a third, and although the number of people over retirement age is expected to remain at its current level of about 9.5 million to the end of the century, the number of the very old will increase significantly. Those over 75 will increase by 620,000 or some 21% between 1979 and the end of the century, with two-thirds of this increase coming by 1986; the number of those over 85 will increase by 50%.[4] The important implications of these trends are an increase in the number of families with three or four generations alive at the same time, and the greater likelihood that families will need to care for elderly relatives (mainly women) for lengthy periods.[5]

Table 1. The dependency ratio*

		1851	1871	1901	1931	1971	2001
Population 0-16 years **	%	35.5	36.2	32.5	24.1	25.5	23.3
16-65 (60)	%	58.4	57.5	61.3	66.3	58.5	60.4
Over retirement age	%	6.1	6.3	6.2	9.2	16.0	16.3
Dependency ratio		0.71	0.74	0.63	0.50	0.71	0.66

Source: adapted from **Social Trends** 9, table 1.2 and **Census 1971** table 5

* Defined as $\dfrac{0\text{-}16 - 65(60)+}{17 - 65(60)}$

** Approximation reflecting changes in the school leaving age.

There is a strong contrast between the overall situation and that of the ethnic minorities. Today just over 3% of the population are of New Commonwealth and Pakistani origin, and in contrast to the indigenous population the New Commonwealth and Pakistani populations are very young; only 10% being over 45 in 1971 compared with 37% for Great Britain as a whole, and 41% being under 15 compared with 24% for Great Britain.[6] The elders in ethnic minorities therefore, form a 'minority within a minority' and the difficulties this creates for them are often overlooked.[7]

Sex ratio

Within the total population, the sex ratio (that is the ratio of males to females — and particularly the ratio of bachelors to spinsters) is one determinant of the number of new marriages that will take place. More boys are born than girls (currently in a ratio of 106 to 100) but differential mortality and migration gradually changes the picture.[8] It is only since 1911 that men have outnumbered women in the under 16 age group, and only from 1961 that this has been true for the 16 to 44 age groups, that is, the age groups in which most marriages take place.

As noted in the Finer Report:
'The distinctiveness of today's situation may be appreciated by recalling how, in mid-Victorian England, almost one-third of the women aged 20 to 44 had to remain spinsters because differential mortality and large scale emigration so depleted the reservoir of men that there were not enough to go round.'[9]

Thus, the more equal sex ratio in the marriageable age groups has increased the potential for marriage within the population. But this more equal sex ratio does not hold at all ages. Currently women constitute 51% of the total population, but in the older age groups (over 75) women outnumber men by more than two to one, as Table 2 shows.

And in contrast to the population as a whole, there is still a substantial imbalance between the sexes among some ethnic minority groups. Pakistani men outnumber women by more than two to one, for example, although a large proportion of recent immigrants have been female.[10]

Table 2. Sex structure of the population by age, Great Britain, 1978

	male		female		total	
age group	000s	%	000s	%	000s	%
0-16	6550	51.3	6207	48.7	12757	100
16-44	10796	50.8	10448	49.2	21244	100
45-59	4729	49.1	4896	50.9	9625	100
60-64	1305	46.8	1486	53.2	2791	100
65-69	1241	44.8	1528	55.2	2769	100
70-74	931	41.2	1327	58.8	2258	100
75-79	551	35.6	996	64.4	1547	100
80-84	249	29.2	603	70.8	852	100
85 and over	129	24.4	400	75.7	529	100
total over 60	4406	42.0	6340	58.0	10746	100
total, all ages	26481	49.0	27891	51.0	54372	100

Source: from OPCS, **Population Projections 1978-2018,** Table 2 Appendix IVC

Marital composition of the population

The more equal sex ratio has enabled more marriages to take place; consequently the proportion of single people in the

13

population has fallen. In 1951, one quarter of the women over 15 had never been married; by 1976 this had fallen to one fifth.[11] However, the total number of people who are married or single at any one time is obviously affected by changes in the age at marriage. The increase in divorce in recent years has been offset to some extent by remarriage, and overall, divorced persons still account for only some 2% of the population. In some of the younger age groups, however, divorcees are more numerous. In 1978, for example, over 4% of men aged 30-39 were divorced (and not remarried), and for women, it was well over 5%.[12] The majority of people of marriageable age are, however, married and will remain so. It is therefore to trends in marriage that we now turn.

Part 2

Marriage

The **number** of marriages in any year can fluctuate widely, and Chart 1 shows both the post-war marriage booms and the effect of the Family Law Reform Act and the Divorce Reform Act 1969. The first of these reduced the age at which marriage could take place without parental consent from 21 to 18 and consequently 'moved forward' some marriages which would probably have taken place later. And the second freed many individuals from long-broken marriages and enabled them to remarry. Indeed these two pieces of legislation focus on the two major trends in marriage over the last century: the decline in the age at marriage, and the greater incidence of marriage breakdown and subsequent remarriage.

Chart 1. Marriages England and Wales, 1900-1976

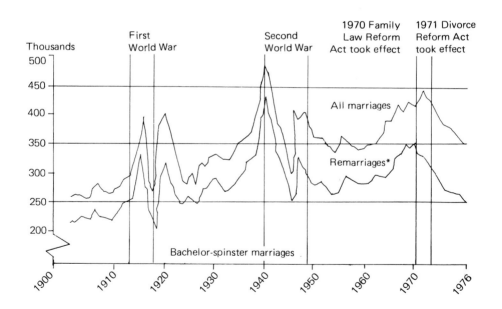

*for at least one partner

Source: Leete, R., **Changing Patterns of Family Formation and Dissolution in England and Wales 1964-76,** HMSO 1979 fig. 3.

There was a gradual upward trend in the **number** of marriages from the Second World War until the early 1970s, after which there was a rapid fall — some 15% in four years. There has been a slight increase since 1976, and currently some 400,000 couples marry each year.

Marriage **rates,** which reflect the number of people in the marriageable age groups, and the frequency of marriage at different ages, rose from the early years of the century to peak in the late 1960s and early 1970s. They have subsequently fallen back, to be nearer the levels current in the 1920s. How can we best explain this trend in marriage patterns, and does the fall in the number and rates of marriage in the 1970s mean that marriage is becoming less popular? People decide not only whether or not to marry, but when they will marry, and Table 3 shows the long term trend towards earlier marriages. This trend was particularly pronounced in the 1960s when nearly 10% of bachelors and 30% of spinsters married in their teens. An additional impetus was the Family Law Reform Act which took effect in 1970. The effect of this Act was a 'borrowing' from marriages in older age groups in later years. In response to the Act, many people who would have married in their twenties, married before they were 21. Some fall in the marriage rates for those aged 20 to 24 in the mid 1970s is therefore a natural consequence of the increase in younger marriages before 1971.[1] From the early 1970s there have also been falls in marriage rates for the youngest age groups. Marriage rates among such young women will be affected by the number who become pregnant and do not have an abortion. The number of women pregnant at marriage has fallen considerably and there has been a reduction in the number of 'forced' marriages.[2]

Alternatively first marriage rates for women over 30 have actually increased in the 1970s, partly as a result of the Divorce Reform Act freeing prospective partners, and partly because of the trend, which has been evident since 1976 towards people marrying later. For men in England and Wales, the median age at marriage rose from 25.4 to 25.6 years between 1977 and 1978, and was 25.8 years during the first half of 1979. For women the corresponding figures are 22.8 years, 23.0 years and 23.1 years.[3]

The answer to both a rising age at marriage and falling marriage rates can be found partly in increasing cohabitation. It has been suggested that: 'At no time in our history has it been so easy to obtain the sexual and other comforts of marriage without troubling to enter the institution'[4] and evidence from

Table 3. Marriage Great Britain, 1901-1978

	1901	1911	1931	1951	1961	1971	1973	1974	1975	1976	1977	1978
Marriages (thousands):												
first marriages for both parties	253	272	307	329	331	357	323	305	296	273	261	269
first marriage for one party only	28	25	28	51	36	54	68	69	70	69	71	75
second (or later) marriage for both parties:												
both divorced	10	9	10	22	21	17	29	31	34	34	37	43
one or both widowed						19	22	21	21	20	19	19
Total	291	307	344	402	387	447	442	426	420	396	394	406
Remarriage* as a percentage of all marriages	13.1	11.4	11.0	18.1	14.6	20.2	27.1	28.3	29.5	31.0	31.0	34.0
First marriages average age of marrying (years)												
bachelors	27.2	27.3	27.4	26.8	25.6	24.6	24.8	24.8	24.9	25.0	25.1**	25.2**
spinsters	25.6	25.6	25.5	24.6	23.3	22.6	22.7	22.7	22.7	22.8	22.9**	22.9**
Remarriages average age of remarrying (years)												
men												
widowed	45.5	46.2	49.2	46.5	49.1	58.7	58.8	58.9	59.1	59.2	59.3	59.3
divorced						39.6	39.2	38.6	38.5	38.3	38.2	38.2
women												
widowed	40.6	41.5	44.3	40.9	42.9	53.2	53.3	53.4	53.5	54.0	54.0	54.0
divorced						35.6	35.4	35.1	35.0	34.8	34.9	34.9

Sources: **Social Trends** 8, table 2.10: **Social Trends** 9, table 2.11; **Social Trends** 11, table 2.9; **Marriage** and **Divorce Statistics** 1978, table 3.5.

* for one or both parties

** these figures refer to England and Wales

the OPCS 'Family Formation' survey shows that growing proportions of couples live together before marriage. Around 10% of women who first married between 1971 and 1975 had lived with their husbands before marriage, compared with 3% who were married for the first time five years earlier.[5] Data from the 1979 General Household Survey suggests that this proportion had risen to 20% for those married in the late 1970s, and in addition, about one in ten single women aged 20 to 29 reported currently cohabiting.[6] Cohabitation is, however, much more likely to precede second or subsequent rather than first marriages, and even when it does not lead to marriage, it is far more common among 'ever married' than single people.[7] On the other hand, the majority of women who are currently cohabiting are still single.

It is worth stressing that Britain is not alone either in experiencing falls in first marriage rates since the late 1960s — similar falls have taken place in the USA, France, Belgium and Germany — nor in rising cohabitation. In both Sweden and Denmark falls in marriage have been accompanied by substantial rises in couples cohabiting and it is estimated that in Sweden among those aged between 18 and 24 there are currently more cohabiting than married couples. Important aspects of these trends are the effect on fertility, and on the legitimacy or otherwise of births. These issues are dealt with in the section on patterns of childbearing.

Falling rates of marriage can therefore be explained to some extent by the changed timing of marriage, and it is premature to regard the decline in marriage rates in the 1970s as signifying the 'end of marriage'. Sharp fluctuations in the proportions of men and women marrying at early ages are often negated by compensating changes later on, and at the present time it is difficult to tell whether the recent decline in marriages will or will not be compensated for in the future.[8] It may well be that cohabitation is becoming more socially acceptable as a prelude to, or even an alternative to, marriage. At present cohabitation appears to be a period of living together **before** marriage -- so that cohabitation and marriage need not be seen as mutually exclusive. Indeed the older women are at marriage the more likely it is that they will have lived with their husbands beforehand.[9] We obviously need to be sensitive to the different ways in which people themselves view their cohabitation. Do they, for example, regard themselves as married or not? In the Family Formation survey cohabiting women were asked this question.

'The answers distinguished clearly between two groups. Those who saw the relationship as a long term commitment, usually including having children and sharing possessions and income, regarded themselves as married. They frequently were unable to marry because one of them was waiting for a divorce. The second group who did not regard themselves as married were much less likely to recognise a long term commitment to their partner, did not share possessions and finance and neither had nor planned to have children. They tended to regard their cohabitation as convenient.'[10]

In this study, 3% of the single, widowed, divorced or separated women reported that they were cohabiting — and of these, two-fifths regarded themselves as married.

On current trends, however, if the marriage patterns of the 1970s are extrapolated, the near universality of marriage could be reversed. There is also a growing disparity in the marriage 'market'. Whereas, on the basis of 1964 marriage patterns 4.5% of females would expect to remain unmarried, and 6.8% of males, the changing sex balance and 1976 marriage patterns suggest that 8.3% of females but 14.2% of males will not marry. The increasing relative scarcity of marriageable women has shown itself in the rise in the median age of marriage for males which is in excess of that for females and in the longer term, the relative surplus of men may affect the relative ages of husbands and wives.[11]

It is, moreover, difficult to generalise from overall marriage patterns since there is considerable variation between social classes. Although there has been an historical trend towards earlier marriage in all socio-economic groups it has gone furthest among manual workers. The Family Formation survey showed that among women in the manual classes, much of the change has taken place in the proportions marrying in their teens. One-fifth of the women in this group born between 1926 and 1935 were married by age 20, compared with two-fifths of those born between 1951 and 1955.[12] In social classes I and II, although there has been a small increase in the proportion married in their teens, there has been a much larger increase in the proportions marrying between 20 and 24. Similarly, the movement towards earlier marriage occurred at different times in different social classes. For the manual classes the increase in teenage marriage occurred among those born between 1936 and 1945, whereas for social classes I and II the increase in marriage between 20 and 24 occurred among those born between 1946 and 1950. These trends have tended, on balance, to widen rather than diminish social class differences,[13] and the differences in marriage are paralleled by those in pre-marital conception, and family size, which are discussed in the next section.

19

Part 3

Fertility and patterns of childbearing

Fertility is the most volatile component of population growth, and it is also difficult to analyse, since it may be viewed in a number of different ways. The total number of live births, although only a crude indicator of fertility, has important implications for service provision, especially for the maternity and education services.[1]

Chart 2. Live births and deaths Great Britain/1855-1975

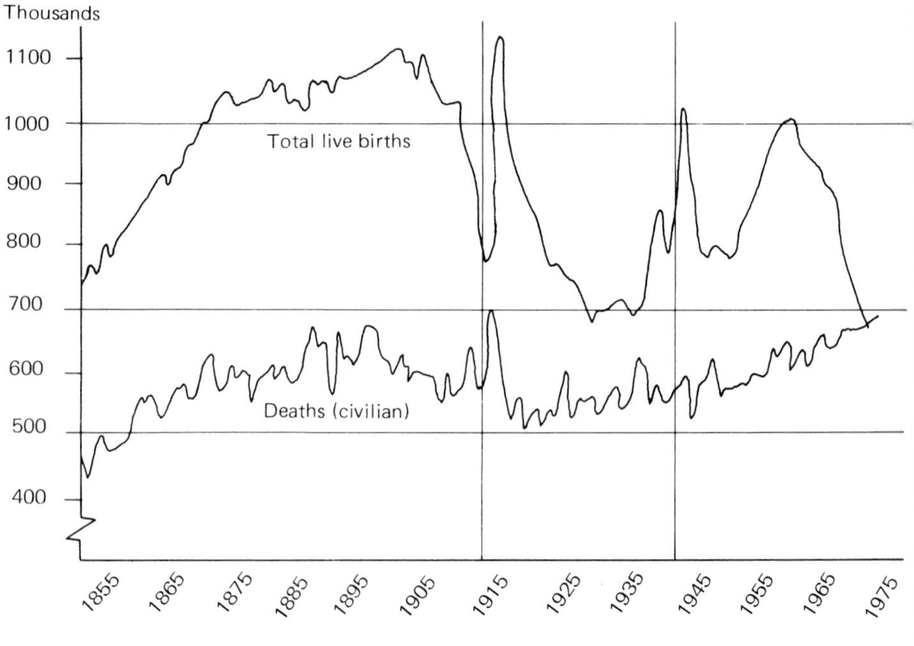

Source: Demographic Review 1977, Fig. 3.1.

In the early years of this century, the annual number of live births was falling steadily, with only a brief interruption immediately after the end of the 1914-18 war. A slight recovery in the latter part of the 1930s was checked by the outbreak of the war of 1939-45. After 1941 the number of live births moved erratically. There have been two 'baby booms', that of 1947 when men demobilised from the armed forces were able to resume their married lives when a peak of 994,000 live births was reached, and that of 1956-65. After 1965 the curve of births began to turn down again, and the decline in the annual number of births between 1965 and 1977 was of the order of 33%.

Table 4. Annual number of births Great Britain, 1946-80

period: mid-year to mid-year	number of births (000s)
1946-51	876
1951-56	768
1956-61	849
1961-66	955
1966-71	904
1971-72	832
1972-73	778
1973-74	724
1974-75	694
1975-76	662
1976-77	630
1977-78	639
1978-79	692
1979-80	715

Source: **Demographic Review 1977,** table 1.2; J L Field, **A Demographic Review 1980** paper presented to British Society for Population Studies Conference, York, September 1980, table 1.2.

Births (in England and Wales) in 1978 were 5% higher than in 1977, and this was followed by an increase of 7% in 1979. These recent increases, however, can be partly explained by changes in the timing of births. In recent years some women have 'postponed' the birth of their first child, and over a longer period there is evidence that childbearing is being 'compressed' into a shorter period within marriage. There can therefore be considerable short term fluctuations, and as Britton notes: 'The experience of the period 1977 to 1979 vividly illustrates the possible volatility in short term fertility trends which, nowadays, is likely when contraceptive practice is more or less widespread and small family sizes predominate, but the timing of births is increasingly affected by short term influences.'[2]

Fertility rates

The number of births in any period is partly a reflection of the number of women in the reproductive age groups (that is 'at risk of pregnancy') their marital status, marriage duration, and the number of previous children. Thus an explanation of changes in the **number** of births needs to be based on an examination of these underlying factors. Demographers therefore supplemen analyses of the **numbers** of births in a given period, with **rates** of birth per 1000 of the population 'at risk', in order to separate behavioural changes from those changes which would be expected from a total population of a given age or marital composition. A useful indicator is the **general fertility rate,** which is the ratio of the number of live births in any year to the number of women of reproductive age alive during that year.

With the exception of the immediate post-war period and the decade of 1956-65, legitimate fertility rates have fallen throughout the twentieth century and now stand at some 90 per thousand per year. Illegitimate fertility rates more than doubled between 1951-5 and 1966-70 to reach 23 per thousand per year in 1968, but had fallen back until 1978 to about 17 per thousand per year.

What these changes in birth rates mean to women of child-bearing age has been noted by Halsey. 'In 1900', he suggests, '**one quarter** of the married women were in childbirth **every year.** Yet thirty years later that proportion was down by one half to one in eight.'[3] Part of the explanation lies in the fall in infant mortality — which has been quite dramatic over the last hundred years. In 1846-50 16.5% of boys and 13.7% of girls would die before their first birthday — and only 7 out of 10 girls would survive to age 15. Today only 1.6% of boys and 1.2% of girls born will die before reaching their first birthday and 98% of girls and 96% of boys born survive to age 15.[4] Parents today, then, can feel much more confident about the survival of their children — and fewer live births are necessary to achieve a given family size.

Obviously, too, parents today want fewer children, and the increase in use of contraception, and the development of more reliable contraceptives has enabled them to plan the size of their families. Also subtly linked to fertility behaviour are the rising aspirations and changing position of women in society.

Patterns of child bearing and family size

The result is that smaller families are now the norm. In the 1870s two-thirds of married women would have five or more children, but by the 1920s the picture had changed so that over two-thirds of married women had two children or fewer, and over the first 50 years of this century the proportion of families with two children had almost doubled. It can be seen from Table 5 that there are two trends at work: there are fewer childless marriages, but far fewer large families.

Table 5. Distribution of family size births occurring to first marriages

number of children	women married in period: 1920-24	1935-39	1956-60*	1961-65*
0	16	15	10	8
1	24	26	17	21
2	24	29	39	41
3	14	15	22	23
4 or more	22	15	12	7
average family size	2.4	2.1	2.1	2.0

*refers to England and Wales, and to marriage durations of 10 years.

Source: **Finer Report** vol I, table 3.8 and K Dunnell, table 4.6.

Indeed today 37% of married couples with dependent children have one child, 41% have two, 15% have three and only 4% have four or more.[5] The two-child family has therefore become more common, and also seems to be the number most frequently desired and expected.[6] Children, then, are growing up in small families, and today 23% of children are in families where they are the only child (at least at present), 44% in a two-child family, 22% in a three-child family and 11% in a four-child family. (The corresponding figures for 1973 were 19%, 38%, 24% and 19%.)[7]

Such a cross-sectional picture may, however, understate the number of families of a given size, since it captures families at different stages in their family building cycle. The majority of births take place within the first ten years of marriage and as noted above, women are now compressing childbearing into a shorter period. There have also been important changes in the timing of first births, which have tended to give an exaggerated picture of the decline in family size. And there are differences too in the social class distribution of family sizes. As Table 6 shows, for women married between 1956 and 1965, 16% of those in social classes IV and V had four or more children compared with only 5% in social classes I and II.[8]

Table 6. Social Class Distribution of Family Size*

number of live births	social class: I+II	IIIN	IIIM	IV+V	total
	%	%	%	%	%
0	8	7	9	9	9
1	17	15	17	18	19
2	47	42	43	33	40
3	23	26	21	24	23
4 or more	5	10	10	16	9
mean number	2.0	2.2	2.1	2.3	2.1

*Proportion of women first married between 1956 and 1965 in different social classes, with different numbers of live births, after ten years of marriage.

Source: K Dunnell, **Family Formation 1976**, table 4.8.

Chart 3. Births: by birthplace of mother Great Britain, 1971 and 1978

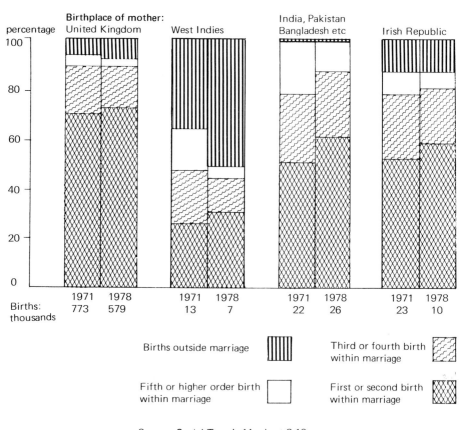

Births: thousands	1971	1978	1971	1978	1971	1978	1971	1978
	773	579	13	7	22	26	23	10

Births outside marriage

Third or fourth birth within marriage

Fifth or higher order birth within marriage

First or second birth within marriage

Source: **Social Trends** 11, chart 3.19.

24

There are also differences in family size between the ethnic minorities and the indigenous population. Some 13% of all births in 1979 were to mothers born outside the UK, compared with about 11% in 1971. Births to mothers from the New Commonwealth and Pakistan were 8% of all births in 1979 and 6% in 1971.[9] The 1971 Census showed that mothers born in the UK had smaller families, on average, than those born in the New Commonwealth and Pakistan. Since 1971, there has been, as Chart 3 shows, a decline in the proportion of higher order (third, fourth and subsequent) legitimate births in all the ethnic minority groups, but women born in the Indian sub-continent are still more likely to have larger families than are those born in either the UK or the West Indies.[10]

Illegitimacy

Nine in every ten children are born within marriage, although illegitimate births as a proportion of all births have risen from about 6% in 1961 to 11% in 1979.[11] The character of illegitimacy is changing: some 55% of illegitimate births in England and Wales in 1979 were registered on the joint information of both parents, compared with 49% five years earlier.[12] And the Law Commission has suggested that the time is ripe for a fundamental review of the law relating to illegitimacy.[13] Where births are registered by both parents one can presume some degree of stability in the union, and the recent increase in illegitimate births must be seen in this light — such births increased by 15% in 1978/79. Part of this increase can, perhaps, be explained by the increasing proportion of illegitimate births to divorced women. An unknown proportion of these women will subsequently marry the father of their child, who himself may be waiting for a divorce.[14] Nonetheless the proportion of illegitimate births is still higher for younger mothers, and has been increasing in these age groups. In 1979 2 in 5 births to women under 20 were illegitimate, and 1 in 8 of those to women between 20 and 24.[15] And one-third of all illegitmate births are to women under 20.[16] West Indian born mothers are, as Chart 3 shows, more likely, and Indian born mothers less likely, than other groups to have children outside formal marriage, and the proportion of births to West Indian born and UK born mothers which are illegitimate has been increasing.

For many women there are two possible alternatives to having an illegitimate child: they can marry the father of the child, or have an abortion. The number of births conceived prior to, and subsequently born within a first marriage has declined dramatically during the 1970s — by over 50% between 1971 and 1977[17] — and it would appear that pregnancy at marriage is much less likely than it used to be. To some extent this reflects the greater use of contraceptives since there is no evidence to suggest that pre-marital sexual activity has declined. Nowadays it seems that when a child is conceived outside marriage, women are more likely to resort to abortion, or failing that to an illegitimate birth, than they are to marry in order to legitimise their child.

Age at first birth

The average age at marriage of men and women marrying for the first time was lower in 1970 than at any period since the start of civil registration. More recently, age at first marriage has risen again. Have there been corresponding changes in the age at which women have their first child? And how do mothers 'space' their families? Has there been a trend to post-ponement of the first child, and if so, how is this likely to affect the number of children women have? Will it lead some couples unwittingly into childlessness?

The majority of studies of childbearing focus on the duration of marriage, but more recently, attention has turned to the age at which childbearing starts. It is clear from Table 7, that the average age of women at their first birth had been falling from the late 1950s until the early 1970s, when it rose again. The age at which women have their first child is obviously not independent of their age at marriage, but within marriage it would seem that much of the choice about the timing of births is exercised in respect of the birth of the first child. Postpone-ment of the start of childbearing was an important factor in the decline in births from the late 1960s to mid 1970s. The median interval between marriage and the birth of the first child rose from 20 months in 1971 to 30 months in 1979.[18] Consequently, whereas between 1965 and 1969 half of all women in their first marriage had had their first child by age 23, by 1979 this was true only at age 24-5.[19] Similarly, whereas in 1971 9 out of 10 first births took place with five years of marriage, this was true of only 8 out of 10 in 1979.[20]

As Table 8 shows, there remain important social class differences in the timing of births: mothers in professional families have their first child later in marriage than other mothers, and those in unskilled workers' families, much earlier. Postponement of childbearing is of course only possible for women not pregnant at marriage, and part of the explanation of the earlier births in social classes IV and V lies in the higher proportion of mothers in these groups who are pregnant at marriage. Even when these are excluded, however, there is a

Table 7. Mean age of women at childbirth: birth order
England and Wales, 1941-78

period/ year of birth	all mater- nities	mean age of women at childbirth			
		first live birth*	second live birth*	third live birth*	fourth live birth*
1941-45	29.1	26.5	29.7	31.8	33.3
1946-50	28.8	26.2	29.2	31.4	33.0
1951-55	28.3	25.4	28.3	30.4	31.9
1956-60	27.8	25.0	27.7	30.0	31.7
1961-65	27.3	24.4	27.0	29.4	31.2
1966-70	26.5	23.9	26.4	28.9	30.9
1971-75	26.2	24.2	26.3	28.6	30.6
1976	26.4	24.7	26.8	28.7	30.5
1977	26.8	24.9	27.0	28.9	30.7
1978	27.1	25.0	27.1	29.1	31.9

*To married women married once only; before 1961 figures relate to maternities.

Source: Population Trends 18, Table I.

Table 8. Birth intervals: by social class*

	Median interval (months) between marriage and first birth (England and Wales)							Median interval (months) between	
	Social class of father								
	Pro- fessional	Inter- mediate occu- pations	skilled occupations non- manual	manual	Partly skilled occu- pations	Un skilled occu- pations	All classes	first and second birth (Great Britain)	second and third birth
1971	32	28	26	19	15	9	20		
1972	33	30	28	20	16	10	22	31	39
1973	35	32	30	22	16	11	24	31	39
1974	37	35	33	23	18	11	26	32	39
1975	38	37	35	25	19	12	28	33	41
1976	39	39	35	26	20	12	29	34	42
1977	42	39	36	27	21	14	30	33	42
1978	44	41	39	28	21	11	31	34	43
1979	44	42	37	27	21	13	30	33	44

*to women married once only

Source: Social Trends 11, Table 2.18.

clear trend for women in non-manual groups to start child-bearing later. The postponement phenomenon has been almost solely confined to social classes I, II and III; for social classes IV and V, the period between marriage and childbearing remained the same throughout the 1960s.[21]

Again, there seems to have been far less of a change in the intervals between first and second, and second and subsequent births, and since families are now rather small, there is no strong reason to believe that delaying the start of childbearing will mean that parents fail to have the number of children they desire. Many women, then, are having their children later than they used to, and are spacing their families so that they are actively involved in childbearing over a fairly short period. This is not true of some ethnic minority mothers, who continue to bear children well into their forties.[22] So whereas for some mothers, childbearing starts later in marriage, in general families are completed earlier than in the past, and in consequence, where the wife has left work to look after children, she is now available for work again at an earlier age.

Table 9. Ideal number of children*

	Year of interview and year of marriage		
	1967	1972	1976
	1955-62	1960-67	1964-71
	%	%	%
0	—	—	1
1	—	1	1
2	23	44	65
3	22	18	17
4	42	28	11
5 and over	8	3	—
Ranges	4	4	2
Don't know/no answer	—	2	2
Mean number	3.4	2.9	2.4
Number of women (=100%)	2,420	1,384	1,667

*Comparison of the percentage distributions and mean numbers of children considered ideal in 1967, 1972 and 1976 for people in this country with no particular worries about money, by women who had been married for up to twelve years.

Source: K Dunnell, **Family Formation 1976**, Table 12.4.

Ideal family size

People have smaller families than they used to partly because more efficient contraceptives are available and are used more extensively, but also because our views about what is an ideal size of family have changed. There is an obvious and important distinction between what one views as ideal for society as a whole, and a personal ideal.

In 1967, a survey of women who had been married for up to twelve years showed that the majority thought that between 3 and 4 children was ideal. A 1976 survey of women married between 1964 and 1971 showed that this had fallen to between 2 and 3 children. And whereas 42% of the earlier sample had seen 4 children as ideal, this is true of only 11% of the latter where, in contrast, 65% viewed the two-child family as ideal.[23] But how many children do women want for themselves? People's views of what is ideal may of course change as they see it becoming more or less likely that they will achieve these ideals. But the 1976 survey showed that women married between 1966-75 reported a personal ideal family size of 2.5 children. This is almost exactly the same as that found in the 1967 survey as a personal ideal which, however, was nearly a whole child less than that thought ideal for society as a whole. So there have been two sorts of convergence taking place. First, women's ideas about what is ideal for them are closer to their ideals for society as a whole, and second, the ideal of the two-child family is far more common now than either the two or four-child family was previously.[24] But important social class differences still remain. Nearly 1 in 5 women in social class V think that four children or more is ideal for society as a whole, in contrast to only 1 in 10 of those in social class I. Their personal ideals are much closer, however, with 21% of the former and 16% of the latter wanting four or more children.[25]

How often do people achieve the size of family they view as ideal? Test-tube babies and multiple births to those taking fertility drugs have hit the headlines recently, and a couple's willingness to consider either adoption or fostering may well be determined by whether they have enough children of their own. In the 'Family Formation' survey, women who were married between 1966 and 1975 wanted on average 2.5 children, but their average expection was just over two. Not only were they expecting to have substantially fewer children than they viewed as ideal, but, even this expectation might be frustrated. Of women married between 1961 and 1965 1 in 5 ultimately had one or no children, whereas only 1 in 12 of those married five years later wanted this number of children. And in the late 1960s and early 1970s far more women wanted large families — more than four children — than expected that they would have them.[26] It may well be therefore that we shall see a growing concern with the problem of too few rather than too many children. Some parents who cannot have the number of children they desire will complete their families by adoption or fostering, which are discussed in Part 7.

Part 4

Marriage breakdown and divorce

For those who see the decline in marriage rates as an indicator of disillusionment with marriage, how much greater must be their concern about the increasing number of divorces? There has been a long term upward trend in the number of civil divorces since statistics first became available in 1857. Prior to 1914, the annual number of divorces in England and Wales never exceeded 10,000, nor 1,000 in Scotland.

There were substantial increases in the wake of both world wars, but the numbers fell back during the 1950s. However, from the early 1960s as Table 10 shows there had been an upward trend, and in 1970 there were more than twice as many divorces as in 1960. The Divorce Reform Act of 1969, which liberalised the grounds for divorce and which took effect in 1971, led to a sharp upward shift in the total number of divorces.

More significant than the number of divorces in any year is the change in the incidence or rates of divorce. 'In Great Britain in 1976 there were approximately 10 divorces per thousand married persons compared with only 2 and 4 per thousand in the periods 1956-60 and 1946-50 respectively; over the last twenty years there has thus been a 400% increase in the divorce rate.'[1]

Divorce rates peak between the ages of 25 and 29 where currently nearly 2% of each sex who are married obtain a divorce each year, and there has been a continuing rise in the divorce rate among the under 25s. There has been a substantial rise in the 1970s in the proportion of divorces occurring in the early years of marriage. 8.3% of the divorces granted in 1978 were to couples who had been married for three years, and a further 8.6% to those who had been married for four years. In 1970 the corresponding figures were 3.9% and 9% respectively.[2] This is partly the result of the fall in marriage age that occurred in the 1960s, meaning that the number of married people aged 20 to 24 at risk of divorce, having married more than three years before, has been growing, and because of the higher risk of divorce of marriages at young ages. Teenage marriages are particularly at risk of breakdown: marriages in which a bride is in her teens are about twice as likely to end in divorce as marriages where the bride is in the age group 20 to 24, and four times as likely as those in which the bride is in the 25 to 29 age group.[3] If the current divorce rates for England and Wales are extrapolated, then the proportion of marriages that would end in divorce after fifteen years would be 33% for women under 20 at marriage, 19% for women 20 to 24 at marriage, 13% for women 25 to 29, and 11% for women 30 to 34 at marriage.[4]

Divorce, however, is not an accurate indicator of the level of marriage breakdown. The number of judicial separations — which may or may not then lead to divorce — is very small, and has declined in comparison with the number of petitions filed for divorce. However, the upward trend is apparent here: from 1955 to 1965 the number doubled, and it more than doubled again from 1965 to 1975.

Not all separations, however, are registered as judicial separations, and until recently the extent of informal separation arrangements was unknown. The 'Family Formation' survey showed that divorce statistics in the 1960s were registering only about half the total breakdowns of marriage. Among women married between 1961 and 1965 for example, 11% had separated by ten years after their marriage, but only 6% had actually divorced.[5] But many of these women will have taken the opportunity to divorce in the 1970s and may now be remarried. Although we do not know how far divorce statistics still understate the true extent of marriage breakdown, it is likely to be less than previously. Nonetheless, it is clear from the 'Family Formation' survey that the pace of marriage breakdown has been increasing. While 6% of women first married between 1956 and 1960 had separated by the end of the tenth year of marriage, this was true of 11% of those married between 1961 and 1965. Of those married in 1966-70, 9% were separated by the end of their fifth year of marriage — only slightly less than the proportion at ten years marriage duration for those married five years earlier.[6]

Many people are rightly concerned about the trends in marriage breakdown, and this prompts the question why do marriages break down, and which marriages are most at risk? An analysis of the complex dynamics of marriage and the causes of marital breakdown are outside the scope of this paper. There are, however, certain factors which seem to be associated with a higher risk of divorce or marriage breakdown. Marriages in which the bride is very young have already been cited as being particularly at risk. Until recently there has been a strong

Table 10: Divorce Great Britain, 1951-1979

	1951	1961	1966	1971	1972	1973	1974	1975	1976	1977	1978	1979
Divorces granted (thousands):												
England and Wales:												
petitions filed (thousands)	38	32	47	111	111	116	132	140	146	168	164	164
decrees nisi granted (thousands)	30	27	41	89	111	107	118	123	131	137	152	142
decrees nisi absolute granted (thousands)	29	25	39	74	119	106	114	120	127	129	144	138
rate per thousand married population	3	2	3.2	6	10	8	9	10	10	10.4	11.6	11.1
Scotland: divorces granted	2	2	4	5	6	7	7	8	8	9	8	8
Great Britain total divorces granted	30.9	26.9	42.9	79.7	124.6	113.6	120.6	128.6	135.4	137.4	152.4	146.2
Percentages of all divorces by duration of marriage (in years) Great Britain												
up to 4	10	11		13	13	16	16	17	18*	18*	18*	19
5 to 9	32	31		30	28	29	30	30	30	30	30	30
10 to 14	24	23		19	18	19	19	18	19	19	19	19
15 to 19	14	14		13	13	13	13	13	13	12	12	12
20 and over	20	21		24	27	23	22	20	20	21	21	20
Total	100	100		100	100	100	100	100	100	100	100	100

*figures refer to England and Wales

Source: **Social Trends** 10, Table 2.11 and OPCS Monitors FM2 80/1 and FM2 81/2 , **Social Trends** 11, Table 2.13.

association between teenage marriage and pre-marital pregnancy, and it is consequently difficult to separate the 'pure' effects of either age at marriage or pregnancy status. The picture also seems to vary with different marriage cohorts. For those married in their teens before 1961, the 'Family Formation' survey showed that the proportions separated at longer marriage durations were the same whether or not the bride was pregnant at marriage.[7] But for women married between 1961 and 1965, the proportion separated after ten years of marriage was 26% for pregnant teenage brides and 15% for non-pregnant teenage brides.[8] However, these results are based on very small numbers and should be treated with caution. Some of this association can probably be explained by the fact that young couples who are forced to marry often have to live with relatives for a period and this imposes strains on the developing relationship. There are also differences in rates of marriage breakdown by social class: where the bride is under 20 at marriage, marriages among manual workers are slightly **less** likely to break down, and where the bride is over 20, slightly **more** likely to break down than in the non-manual groups.[9]

The complexity of the factors which pre-dispose some marriages to end in divorce is emphasised in the study by Thornes and Collard.[10] They comment that research in both Britain and the United States has failed to isolate any one, or even several, dominant variables which distinguish those marriages which end in divorce from those which continue. Consequently 'it therefore seems probable that the variables which characterise those who divorce will not only be both numerous and subtle in their interaction with one another, but also likely to be indicative of a wide variety of differing pathways to divorce.'[11]

Their study supported previous findings that couples from dissimilar backgrounds were more prone to divorce, as were those whose period of courtship had been short. Teenage marriage, pre-marital pregnancy and break-ups during courtship were also found to be important contributory factors. The reasons for and effects of childlessness within marriage were not explored in this particular study, but this is obviously an important area.

Divorce and children

There is no doubt that the process of divorce can have traumatic effects on the children of a divorcing couple, and there is considerable debate about whether couples do, or should 'stay together for the sake of the children'. Quantitative studies cannot really answer this question, although some indication of the number of children involved in divorce can be gleaned from official statistics. The proportion of divorces involving dependent children has increased from 57% to 60% between 1971 and 1978, and in 1978 a further 10% involved independent children. This means that in that year nearly 86,000 couples who divorced had children under 16 — a total of nearly 163,000 children. Within this total over 30,000 couples had a youngest child below school age; indeed 37,000 children or 23% of all the dependent children involved in divorces in that year were under five.[12] This compares with 26% in 1971. The total number of children involved in divorces has risen in recent years, from 82,000 in 1971 to 163,000 in 1978, but the average number of dependent children per divorcing couple has fallen slightly, reflecting the increasing number of couples having two children, and the decline in the number with three or more children.[13] The current trend for a higher proportion of divorces to occur in the early years of marriage, and the trend to delayed first births may mean that in the future fewer divorces will involve children.

The question of whether couples remain together for the sake of the children could be interpreted in a number of ways: do couples wait until the children have grown up? In this case there would be a rise in divorce rates at longer durations of marriage. Are childless marriages more prone to divorce than those where there are children? Or are couples with larger families more likely to stay together than those with smaller families?

Leete has shown that divorce rates in fact decline with increasing duration of marriage, tending to reject the idea that couples postpone divorce until the children have grown up. By an approximate comparison of the family size of married and divorcing couples in 1976, he shows that childlessness amongst divorcing couples exceeded that amongst those who remained married by 12% after three years of marriage, 14% after five years, 13% after seven years and 8% after nine years. In interpreting this evidence, however, it needs to be recognised that each divorcing couple will inevitably have been separated for an unknown and variable length of time before their divorce.[14] On the assumption that the marriages of the divorced ended two years prior to their actual divorce, the family size distribution of divorcing couples should be compared with those of a marriage cohort two years later. On this basis the difference in family size becomes much less significant, with 31% of divorcing couples who were married in 1968-69 having no children compared with 29% of married couples who remained married from the 1970-71 marriage cohort. Any correlation of childlessness with marriage breakdown, therefore, seems weak and is more likely to reflect differences in the duration of marriage.

There is an apparent tendency for couples who divorce to have smaller families than those who remain married but 'it is impossible to judge from the available statistics whether marriages with children are more stable, and hence less prone to divorce; it may be for instance, that couples in relatively unstable marriages hesitate to have a child merely because of its instability. Moreover, it is impossible to say how far such a tendency is off-set by the efforts of those couples who beget children simply in the hope of staving off divorce.'[15]

We have seen that the number of children involved in divorce has grown but the average number of children per divorcing couple has stayed remarkably constant. Thus the fact that more children have been affected simply reflects the increasing number of divorces. However, this means that between 1970 and 1976 the number of children involved in divorce in a year has risen from 6 in every thousand children to 13 in every thousand. Chart 4 shows these trends for various age groups. As yet there are no reliable estimates of how many children could expect, during their childhood, to experience their parents' divorce. However, a combination of available statistics does suggest an approximation. Currently, one in four marriages are likely to end in divorce, some 60% of which will involve dependent children; and the number of children involved in divorce each year is now 13 per thousand. Thus we might expect that between one in five and one in six children born today may witness their parents' divorce before they reach sixteen.

Chart 4. **Children of divorced couples** per 1000 children

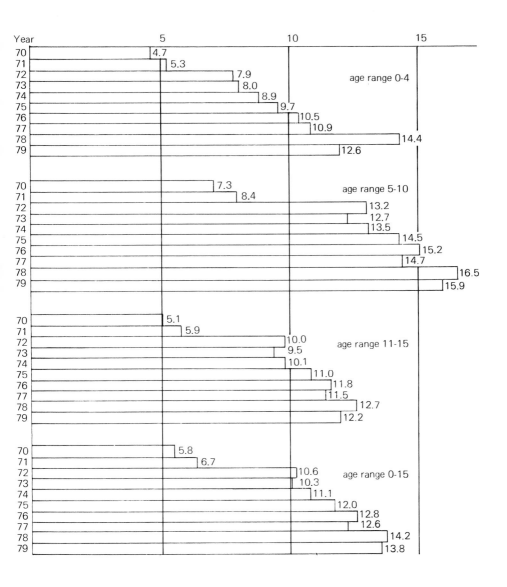

Source: R Leete, **Changing Patterns of Family Formation and Dissolution**, Table 4.2. Updated from OPCS Monitor FM2 81/2

Part 5 **One-parent families**

Perhaps one of the most often identified consequences of the increase in marriage breakdown is the rising proportion of one parent families in the population. Although all children have two parents — and indeed the relationship and respective rights and duties of each of these is the subject of much current debate — at any one time a number of children will have only one parent living at home.

Prior to the investigation of the Finer Committee, information about the number and circumstances of one parent families was very sparse.[1] Estimates produced for the Committee suggested that something like 620,000 families in Great Britain were one parent families in 1971, but this was subsequently revised downwards (to 570,000) to take account of supplementary information about the extent of cohabitation. By 1976 the number had grown to 750,000, and the National Council for One Parent Families estimates that there were in 1980 some 920,000 one parent families with the care of about one and a half million children.[2] About 1 in 8 families, then, is headed by a lone parent, and there is some evidence to suggest that slightly more West Indian families have only one parent — 13% in 1976 compared with 9% of all families — whereas only 1% of Asian families was headed by a lone parent at that date.[3]

Reliable estimates of the number of families and children living in one parent families have been difficult to produce, partly because of the lack of administrative statistics covering some of the routes into and out of one parent status, which are shown in chart 5, and secondly because of limitations in the 1971 Census information which is available. The best estimates available of the number and composition of one parent families are a composite from three major sources — the Census, the General Household Survey (GHS), and figures derived from the administration of other social security benefits — particularly Child Benefit. (The nature and limitations of these sources is described in some detail in Appendix 2.) Central to the issue of estimating the number of one parent families is the need to specify exactly what is meant by a one parent family. The Finer Committee defined a one parent family as 'a father or mother living without a spouse (or not cohabiting), with his or her never-married dependent child or children aged either below 16 or 16 to 19 and undergoing full-time education'. Thus this definition both excludes cohabiting parents, and parents whose children are no longer dependent. There are of course, very real difficulties in defining when cohabitation begins or ends, as a persistent debate in the administration of supplementary benefits shows,[4] and an analysis of 1975-1977 GHS data suggested that only about one half of the hundred thousand one parent families in the Census which had been identified as living in households containing a person of the opposite sex were in fact cohabiting.[5] Furthermore, in the case of cohabitees, this definition implies that the 'father' does in fact support the mother and her children — a situation which is often **assumed** to hold but which has been shown in practice not to do so.[6]

Chart 5. Formation and ending of one parent families

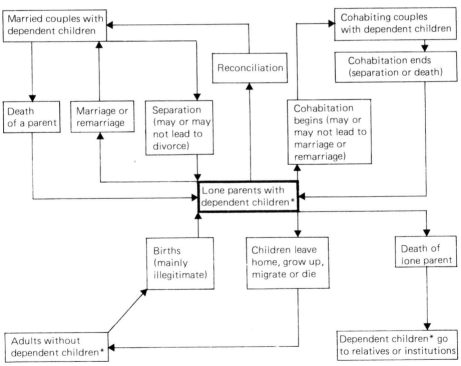

*A dependent child in this context is a person aged under 16, or between 16 and 19 and undergoing full-time education.

Source: R Leete, 'One parent families: Numbers and characteristics' **Population Trends** 13, 1978, fig. 1.

Since its inception in 1971, much valuable information about one parent families has come from the GHS. Overall the number of one parent families has been increasing at about 6% a year, and as Table 11 shows there has been a disproportionate increase in the number of divorced and single mothers.

Table 11. Families by type and, for lone mothers, marital status
Great Britain, 1971-1979

Families with dependent children*

Family type	1971 – 73	1972 – 74	1973 – 75	1974 – 76	1975 – 77	1976 – 78	1977 – 79
	%	%	%	%	%	%	%
Married couple	90.8	90.4	89.7	89.1	88.8	88.4	88.1
Lone mother	8.0	8.3	8.9	9.4	9.8	10.3	10.6
Lone father	1.2	1 3	1.4	1.4	1.3	1.3	1.3
Lone mother							
-married	1.0	1.0	0.9	1.0	1.0	1.0	0.9
-single	1.2	1.3	1.3	1.4	1.5	1.6	1.7
-widowed	1.8	1.8	1.9	1.9	2.0	2.0	1.9
-divorced	1.9	2.1	2.6	2.9	3.2	3.6	3.8
-separated	2.1	2.2	2.2	2.3	2.1	2.1	2.3
Total: lone parent	9.2	9.6	10.3	10.8	11.1	11.6	11.9

*Dependent children are persons aged less than 16, or aged 16-18 and in full-time education.

Source: GHS Monitor 80/I. Table 3.

The increase in the number of single mothers is consistent with the fact that, while until 1978 the number of illegitimate births was falling, a smaller proportion of unmarried women who became pregnant and continued with their pregnancy went on to marry, or offered their child for adoption. And the increased proportion of divorced lone mothers reflects the substantial increase in the number of divorces previously described. Today, 1 in 9 single parents is a lone father, 1 in 7 is an unmarried mother, 1 in 6 is a widowed mother, 1 in 3 is a divorced mother, and a further 1 in 5 is a 'separated' mother.[7] It would be wrong therefore to view one parent families as a homogeneous group, and the circumstances through which parents and children enter a one parent family can have an important impact on their experience of life in this type of family.[8]

We need to be sensitive, then, both to differences between one parent and two parent families, and within the one parent family group. Lone fathers are generally slightly older (median age of forty-two) and lone mothers slightly younger (median age of thirty-five) than the heads of married-couple families (median age of thirty-eight). But the median age of lone mothers varies from twenty-five for single lone mothers to thirty-five for divorced and separated mothers and to forty-seven for widowed mothers.[9] Indeed 60% of widowed mothers are over forty-five compared with only 7% of single mothers and 13% of divorced mothers. Since remarriage is more likely for younger women, on this basis alone widows are less likely to remarry than those who have been divorced.

On average lone parents have slightly smaller families than two parent families. Whereas the average number of children in a lone father family is the same as for that of married couples (1.9), for lone mothers it is 1.7. Indeed over half (52%) of lone mothers only have one child and a further 31% have two. Within the lone mother group, single mothers have the smallest number of children with 80% having just one child whereas divorced and separated mothers have the largest families, an average of two children. On average, too, fewer one parent families contain a child under five, this is true of only 30% of families headed by a lone mother and of only 6% of families headed by a lone father. In contrast 29% of married couple families contained a youngest child between ten and fifteen, but this was true of 50% of lone father families.[10]

Although we talk about single or lone parent families, a number of such parents and their children live with others. Indeed some 15% of lone parents live with their own parents and a further 4% live with relatives. Predictably a much higher proportion of unmarried mothers live with others, some 49% in 1978.[11] For many this reflects housing problems but it also means that children will have other 'family' figures around.

While there has been growing recognition of the increased numbers of one parent families, the implications of current trends are often underestimated. A very serious limitation of many existing statistics is that they are cross-sectional — that is they show the situation at one point in time. Such estimates appreciably understate the cumulative number of parents (and children) in the population who have ever lived, or will live in a one parent family at some time. Until more adequate information is available on the 'risk' of becoming a one parent family it seems certain that this issue will be under-appreciated. Although it is perhaps dangerous to cite America as a precedent, estimates emerging from the Bureau of the Census suggest that for a child born in 1977 the chances of being in a one parent family at some point before his sixteenth birthday is as high as 1 in 2.[12] For Britain some evidence on a longitudinal basis is now becoming available. The National Child Development Study of a cohort of children born in 1958 showed that at age seven, 3% of the sample were living in a one parent family. By age eleven, this had risen to 5% and by age sixteen it was as high as 9%.[13] But there was evidence of considerable movement in and out of one parent family situations, and over 12% of the children in the study had been living in a one parent family on one of these three occasions. Given that there are others who will have been in one parent families **between** the interview dates, even the 12% figure is an underestimate.[14]

More recently the Child Health and Education Study at the University of Bristol has shown that just under 5% of the sample of children were born to unsupported women. Five years later in 1975 just under 6% of the children were living in a one parent family. At some time during their first five years, however, a much larger proportion of children — nearly 11% in all — had experienced an episode of living in a one parent family.[15] Although the definition of what constitutes one parent status differs in these studies it would seem that children born in 1970 are more likely to experience family changes at an earlier age than children born in 1958.[16]

It is plausible that the family situation of children in some one parent families is more changeable than that of those in two parent families. The follow up study of illegitimate children in the National Child Development Study showed that illegitimate children were three times more likely to experience a change in parental care between the ages of seven and eleven than either legitimate or adopted children (15% compared with 5%).[17] And a smaller study of illegitimate children which compares the experience of these children with that of a control group shows a similar picture. Fifteen percent of both the control and illegitimate children had absent fathers at the time of interview, but in the previous ten year period, only 20% of the control group had experienced two 'care' situations, whereas this was true of all the illegitimate children. Indeed, 15% of these children had been in three care situations, 5% in four and 10% in five.[18]

For some children the period in a one parent family may be relatively short but we still know too little about the length of time parents and children spend as a one parent family. Evidence from the National Children's Bureau showed that three-quarters of children at age seven being cared for by their mothers alone were still in this situation at eleven years of age, and that only one mother in five was remarried or cohabiting.[19] Over a third of the children who had been born to unsupported mothers in the Child Health and Education Study were still members of a one parent family at age five.[20] This also suggests that for some children living with one parent is a long term experience. On the other hand, although more than 12% of the 1958 cohort experienced a one parent state at one interview date, only 0.3% were with their mothers alone at all four ages.[21] The duration of lone parenthood may well be related to the age of the parent, and that of the child, and some of these issues are discussed in the section on remarriage.

Finally, national figures of the number and type of one parent family can be misleading. In Inner London, for example, nearly one family in three is headed by a single parent, and in the catchment area for particular schools, the number can be higher still.[22] These differences have obvious implications for the provision of services at a local level, some of which are discussed later.

Lone parents' incomes

Any description of one parent families would be incomplete without mention of their financial circumstances. As a group, lone parents in general are less well off than two parent families and rely far more heavily on state benefits — notably supplementary benefits and Family Income Supplement (FIS) than their two parent counterparts. The risk of poverty amongst one parent families is high, and there may be little to be gained by combining part-time work with receipt of benefit. Lone mothers are therefore often faced with the choice of bringing up their children at the levels of living provided through the supplementary benefit system, or are forced to work longer hours than mothers in two parent families to achieve a decent standard of living for the children. If they do rely on supplementary benefits, new relationships may be hampered by the knowledge that they forfeit benefit in their own right if they begin to cohabit. Separated and divorced women often face very real difficulties in obtaining the maintenance which they have been awarded by the courts from their (ex)husbands. Social security provisions are failing to cope adequately with increasing marriage breakdown, and the strains which this inadequacy imposes on lone parents is an important part of understanding the reality of life for such parents and their children.

Part 6

Re-marriage

Today some 34% of new marriages involve remarriage for one or both spouses. In 1901 it was only 13.1%, in 1951, 18.1%, and by 1971 it was still only 20.2%. There was a sharp rise between 1971 and 1973 to 27.1% reflecting the Divorce Reform Act, and the increase in remarriage is almost entirely due to the increase in divorced persons remarrying.[1] Indeed as Chart 6 shows remarriages involving one divorced spouse are by far the largest component of all remarriages, and within that, remarriages involving both spouses who have been divorced are the largest single component. Thus 11% or about 1 in 9 of all new marriages involve both spouses who have been divorced.[2] This reflects both the fact that there are, at younger ages, far more divorced than widowed people, and that whereas widowhood is an involuntary status, prospective remarriage for one or both parties is frequently a reason for divorce. On the basis of current trends, around 1 in 5 men will have been remarried by the year 2000, and a slightly smaller proportion of women will have entered a second or later marriage. The likelihood of remarriage varies with age, and is particularly high at ages under 30. More than a third of the divorced persons under 30 remarry during a year — suggesting that something like 80% of this group will remarry within five years.[3] Indeed the OPCS record linkage study of divorce and remarriage showed that of a thousand couples divorcing in 1973 in only 233 couples had neither party remarried by the end of 1977. In 34% of the remaining 777 cases, both parties had remarried, in 27% the wife only had remarried and in 37% the husband only had remarried by this time.[4] Given that divorce often occurs in order for a remarriage to take place, it was to be expected that a higher proportion of the eventual remarriages would take place fairly quickly after divorce, and this proved to be the case. Indeed, about a third of both husbands and wives who had remarried by the end of 1977 had done so within three months of divorce, and by the end of the first year after divorce about 60% of both men and women who remarried within the following four-and-a half years had already done so.

Chart 6. Marriage and remarriage: a typology England and Wales, 1978

A. all new marriages: Proportion of bride and grooms who married spouses of various marital statuses

groom \ bride	single	divorced	widowed
single	65%	8%	0.7%
divorced	9%	11%	1.0%
widowed	0.7%	1.0%	2.0%

Source: Marriage and Divorce Statistics 1978, Table 3.7. .

B. remarriages 1978

Proportion of divorcees or widow(er)s who married:

	bride	groom
bachelors/spinsters	36	38
widow(er)s	14	14
divorcees	50	48

Source: Marriage and Divorce Statistics 1978, Table 3.2.

The extent of remarriage amongst the divorced is often taken to signify that while people may become disillusioned with a particular marriage, they are not becoming disillusioned with marriage as an institution. While this is obviously true in one sense, one could ask whether those divorcees who had previously been married longer would be more or less likely

45

to remarry than those married for shorter periods. The record linkage study threw some light on this question — and there is an interesting difference between the sexes. For women the length of previous marriage is inversely related to the chances of remarriage, but this does not seem to hold for men. In contrast, age at divorce is strongly related to chances of remarriage for both men and women.

It is also often suggested that divorced wives with dependent children might be less likely to remarry, because of the reluctance of a man to take on the responsibility of a ready-made family. This suggestion was not confirmed by the record linkage study — if anything, at younger ages, the proportion who remarried was slightly higher among those with children. For those divorced over the age of 40, however, there was a greater likelihood that those without children would remarry, compared with those with children. Obviously, though such results need to be treated with great caution. We know, for example, that second or subsequent unions are far more likely to take the form of cohabitation than are first time unions and, indeed, this has been suggested as an explanation of the rise in rates of illegitimate births from 1977 onwards.[5] Equally, we do not know how many of the divorcees who do not remarry would wish to do so were their prospective spouses free to do so. One factor which did seem to influence the proportion of women who remarried was the age of the youngest child at the time of the divorce. Women whose youngest child was under ten years old remarried more often than those whose children were older, or indeed than those who had no children. One interpretation of this is that it may reflect the attitudes of children towards step-parents — older children may be more reluctant to accept them — and this in turn could affect the mother's attitude to remarriage. On the other hand it could reflect the fact that women who have young children may themselves be younger than those with older children, and therefore be more likely to remarry in any event.

The increasing number of remarriages involving divorced people, particularly divorced women who are more likely to have custody of the children, has led to an increase in the number of families in which one of the parents will not be the child's natural parent. The problems and issues surrounding step-parenting are only just being recognised and researched.[6] A particularly interesting issue is that of fertility amongst remarried couples.[7] Is it the case, that a couple, both of whom may have children from a previous marriage in the household will still wish to have 'a child of their own'? Births to remarried women are, predictably, forming an increasing proportion of all births. In 1979 they accounted for 5.8% of births compared with 5.3% three years earlier, and only 2.5% in 1971.[8] And it is known that the age specific fertility rate is greater among remarried women (at ages between 20 to 29), than among women married once only. Burgoyne and Clark have suggested that it is important to distinguish between the 'social' parenting of children in a remarriage, anc 'blood' parenting.[9] If the rewards from social parenting are insufficient, they argue, then the couple is more likely to want children of their own, and this may be more important for mothers than for fathers. Whether such remarried women will want to have more children or not is currently the subject of some research. However, should they decide to do so the majority of them will still have a considerable part of their child-bearing years ahead of them. In 1979 the median age for all divorced women who remarried was thirty-three years, and the lower quartile was 28.1 years. Thus, provided their new marriages last until they reach 45, a quarter of these remarried women will have seventeen years of potentially fertile life in their second marriages and one half will have twelve years.[10]

Re-divorce

Do people whose marriages break down get it right next time? It is not possible at present to say whether remarriages are more prone to divorce than are first marriages. But the proportion of divorces involving re-divorce for one or both partners has risen from under 9% in 1966 to 16% in 1979, and for divorces where both partners have been divorced before it has risen from 1.4 to 5.2%.[11] Today, then, 1 in 20 divorces involves re-divorce for both partners.

Part 7

Reconstituted or blended families

Increasing divorce, coupled with increasing remarriage, and the fact that the majority of divorces involve children, mean that a growing number of families will be 'reconstituted' or 'blended'. For some, the period as a one parent family will be a short transitional period between one two parent family and a new family with a new 'parent' figure and new brothers and sisters. For others it may last much longer. Again, we know too little about the situation of children in reconstituted families, and the complexity of relationships in such families has not been given the prominence it deserves.

The number of children who no longer live with both their natural parents increases as children grow older. The National Child Development Study showed that by age seven, 8% of children were not living with both natural parents. By eleven years, this had risen to over 11% and by sixteen, some 16% of children were no longer living with both their natural parents.[1]

The likelihood that children will live in families without one or other of their natural parents seems to be increasing. The 1946 National Survey of Health and Development showed that by age fifteen, 11% of children were no longer in the care of both natural parents, whereas for the 1958 cohort, as we have noted, the figure was 16% — or 50% higher — when they were one year older.[2]

And in the Child Health and Education Study almost 3% of the children were living in step-families at age five, in addition to the 6% who at that time were in a one parent family — suggesting that some 8% or more of the children were no longer living with both natural parents.[3]

In the majority of cases where marriages end in divorce mothers are given the custody of their children. For most children, therefore, the new parent figure will be a new father, but the balance between children not living with their natural mother or father changes with age of the child. In the National Child Development Study, for example, six and a half times as many children at age seven had 'lost' their natural fathers as had 'lost' their natural mothers. At eleven, there were only four and a half times as many.[4] Nonetheless, as Chart 7 shows, at sixteen, there are still substantially more children who had 'lost' their natural fathers (13%) than had 'lost' their natural mothers (5%).[5] For a number of children there will be no regular father or mother figure, and we can only guess at the uncertainties and difficulties this creates for young children.

Chart 7. Parent figures of 16-year-old children living in families without one or both natural parents Great Britain, 1974

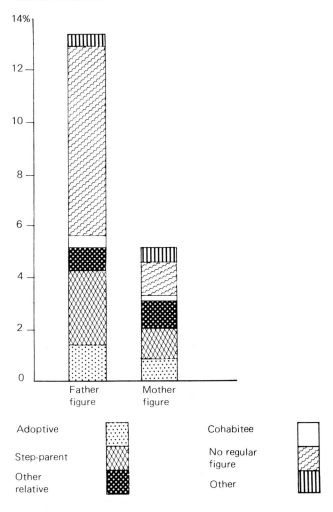

Percentage of all children in families

Source: CPRS, CSO: **People and Their Families,** Chart 3e. From: Britain's Sixteen Year Olds, National Children's Bureau, 1976

49

In some cases where a mother or father remarries the new 'parent' will adopt the child, but such cases are now covered by the Children Act 1975 which is discussed below.

Adoption and fostering

From the mid-1950s when about 13,000 adoptions took place every year, the numbers grew rapidly to a peak of 25,000 in 1968 since when they have fallen back sharply, returning by the late 1970s to the level of the early 1950s.[6]

Chart 8. The changing pattern of adoption

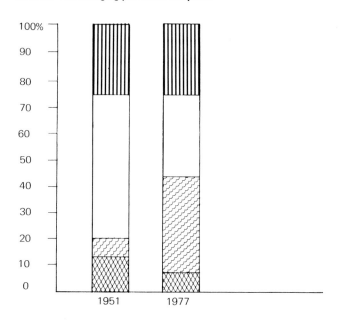

Illegitimate child: one parent natural.

Illegitimate child: neither parent natural.

Legitimate child: one parent natural

Legitimate child: neither parent natural

Source: From R Leete, **Trends in Adoption 1951-1977, Population Trends** 14.

Adoption can be classified either by the status of the adoptive child, or by the status of the adoptive parents. Thus there are four categories: a legitimate child adopted by a couple neither of whom is his natural parent (for example, an orphan); a legitimate child adopted by a couple, one of whom is his natural parent (for example, on the remarriage of the parent following widowhood or divorce); an illegitimate child, adopted by a couple neither of whom is his natural parent; and, an illegitimate child, adopted by a couple one of whom is his natural parent (for example, when an unmarried mother marries a man who is not the father of her child). Chart 8 shows the share of adoptions granted in 1951 and 1977 which were of each type. The chart shows that in the 1950s non-parental adoption of illegitimate children dominated the whole pattern of adoption, whereas in the late 1970s parental adoption of legitimate and illegitimate children taken together accounted for the majority of adoptions.

Parental adoptions of legitimate children increased in importance up to the mid 1970s, reaching a peak of over 9,000 in 1975. This reflected the growth in remarriage, where a step parent would adopt his spouse's child. The Houghton Committee considered that a child's links with one of its natural parents should not necessarily be severed on the remarriage of the other parent, and this philosophy was enshrined in the 1975 Children Act which came into operation in 1976. The Act did not remove the power to grant adoption orders in these cases, but it gave the option of varying custody orders under the Matrimonial Causes Act 1973 if the Court felt this to be more appropriate. This type of adoption has fallen in number from 9,000 in 1975 to less than 5,000 in 1977, and, although practice seems to vary, this fall may continue.

Non-parental adoptions of illegitimate children — which are the type of adoption most likely for those without children of their own — rose with the rise in illegitimate births in the 1950s and fell again in the late 1960s. But the decline in adoptions in later years has been much steeper than the decline in illegitimate births. Adoption agencies still face more people wanting to adopt babies than there are babies available, and so the most likely explanation of this trend is that a higher proportion of illegitimate children are kept by their mothers. Adoptions by parents and by non-parents tend to take place at different ages: the rates of adoption by non-parents start from a sharp peak during the first year of life and then rapidly level, (that is, non-parents prefer to adopt babies); parental adoptions take place later in the child's life, but with about half this type of adoption in any year being of a child aged five or over. Again these trends seem to be changing: it is estimated that some 25% or more of illegitimate births are to parents in stable unions,[7] and a comparison of illegitimate children born at various dates shows that fewer are being adopted in the early years.

Since illegitimate children can be increasingly seen as 'wanted children' it is more and more likely that adoption and fostering services will be concerned with children with special needs — handicapped children, children of mixed race or from the ethnic minorities.

Adoption may be preceeded by fostering, or foster care may be undertaken on a short term basis. Those traditionally involved in fostering — older married women whose own children have grown up — are now more likely to be going out to work, and it has been suggested that since 1961 one and three-quarter million married women have been lost from the pool of the economically inactive, and therefore from the pool of potential foster parents.[8] In consequence, a number of those previously excluded from fostering — single men for example — are now able to do so.

It is important to remember, then, that in an increasing number of families one or other parent may not be the child's natural parent, and that children may face periods of adjustment to new parents and new siblings.

Part 8 Old age and the extended family

Many people, when talking about families, mean families with children, and they pay far less attention to the other end of the life cycle. Yet the position of elderly people in our society will be one of the major challenges for social policy for the remainder of the century.[1]

We have shown that the proportion of the population over retirement age has been rising, reflecting an 'ageing' of the population. This ageing of the population is partly a result of the decline in the birth rate, and partly of the increased expectation of life which is itself the result of changes in mortality rates, which have fallen throughout the last century. The fall in death rates has not been evenly spread throughout the period (being particularly rapid in 1896-1900 and 1946-50), and has been far more pronounced for childhood and early adult life than for the middle aged and elderly. The improving health of the population has therefore meant that young people's chances of reaching the older age groups have improved. A boy born in 1977 could expect to live to nearly seventy, and a girl to seventy-six. In 1901, their life expectancy would have been forty-eight and fifty-two years respectively. But, as table 12 shows, for those who do survive to old age, the expectation of life has increased relatively little.

What do these changes mean for families? Compared with earlier periods, today's children are very likely to have grandparents alive during much of their childhood and a significant proportion will have one or more great-grandparents too. This affects the meaning of 'family' for children and also means that large numbers of the elderly have potential contacts with a significant number of family members. A cross-national survey carried out in 1962 showed that, of the elderly who had children, 89% also had grandchildren. The survey also showed that 23% of the elderly with children also reported having great-grandchildren — 26% of elderly women and 18% of elderly men.[2] A more recent survey suggests that some 60% of the very elderly (over 75) had grandchildren, and it is probable that the number of families with four generations alive will be higher today. It is also true that a significant proportion of the elderly have far **fewer** potential family

53

Table 12. Expectation of life: at birth and at specific ages United Kingdom

	Males						Females					
	1901	1931	1951	1961	1971	1977	1901	1931	1951	1961	1971	1977
Further number of years which a person could expect to live:												
at birth	48.0	58.4	66.2	67.9	68.8	69.9	51.6	62.4	71.2	73.8	75.0	76.0
at age:												
1 year	55.0	62.1	67.5	68.6	69.2	69.9	57.4	65.1	72.1	74.2	75.2	75.8
5 years	55.4	60.0	63.9	64.9	65.4	66.1	57.8	63.0	68.4	70.4	71.4	72.0
30 years	34.6	38.1	40.2	40.9	41.3	42.0	36.9	41.0	44.4	46.0	47.0	47.5
45 years	23.2	25.5	26.4	26.9	27.3	27.8	25.3	28.2	30.6	31.9	32.7	33.2
60 years	13.4	14.4	14.8	15.0	15.3	15.7	14.9	16.4	17.9	19.0	19.8	20.2
70 years	8.4	8.6	9.0	9.3	9.5	9.6	9.2	10.0	10.9	11.7	12.5	12.8
80 years	4.9	4.8	4.8	5.2	5.5	5.5	5.4	5.4	5.8	6.3	6.9	7.0

Source: Social Trends 11, Table 8.1.

contacts: evidence from different sources suggests that approximately a third of the elderly have no or no surviving children at all.[3]

The period of rapid increase in the number of elderly people is now over. But as Chart 9 shows the number of very elderly people will increase as a proportion of the elderly population. Between now and the end of the century there will be 20% more people over seventy-five and 50% more over eighty-five. As Chart 10 shows the majority of these elderly people will be women; indeed three-quarters of those aged over eighty-five are women. While increasing age cannot be equated automatically with increasing dependency, the proportion of people with some degree of disability rises sharply above the age of seventy-five.[4]

Chart 9. Elderly people: by age group Great Britain

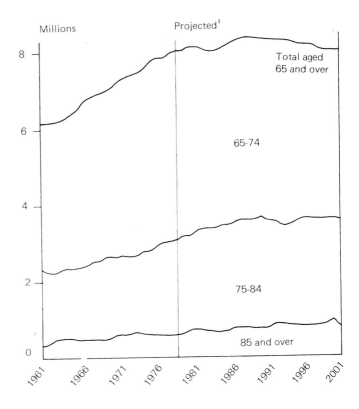

[1] 1979-based projections

Source: **Social Trends** 11, chart 3.11.

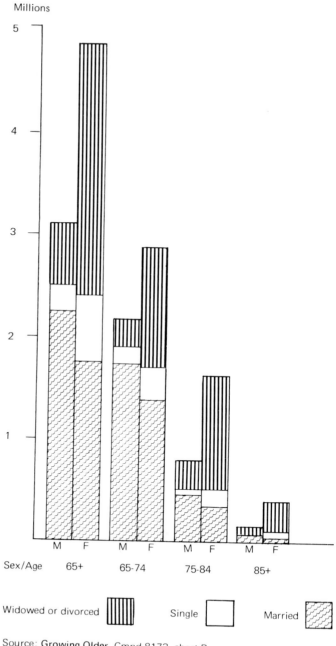

Source: **Growing Older**, Cmnd 8173, chart B

Thus the need for help and support for elderly people will rise sharply in the next two decades. Who gives this help and what do we know about the family life of old people?

Since 1961 the proportion of households which are 'no family' households and in which one or more persons is over retirement age, has risen from 10% to 17%. For one person pensioner households the increase is even greater — from 7% to 15%.[5] As Table 13 shows, although only one-third of the elderly living in private households live alone, this rises to over 50% for women aged over seventy-five.[6]

Whereas the majority of elderly men are still living with their wives (73%), this is true for only a minority of women (36%). And, as one would expect, the proportion living with their wives or husbands declines with age.

As they get older, those who remain in private households are more likely to live with 'others' — and the vast majority of these 'others' are relatives. Three-quarters of women over eighty-five who are living without their spouses but with 'others', are living with their children or children-in-law, as are four-fifths of such men. As an early report from the General Household Survey noted 'this is because old people, faced by widowhood and a decline in self-sufficiency, often return to live with their children and their children's families'.[7] The majority of the elderly, then, either live alone or in families: only 2% live in residential institutions, although about 10% are likely to enter a residential home at some stage in their lives.[8] A higher proportion of elderly **women** live alone — but those over eighty-five are slightly less likely to do so than those between seventy-five and eighty-four.

Living alone, or in a 'no family' household, however, does not necessarily mean that the elderly do not benefit from or contribute to family life. Living near relatives is often as important as living with them. Although there have developed a number of 'retirement areas' near the coast, in which visits from younger relatives may be less frequent, a high proportion of the elderly who moved to those areas did so to be near relatives.[9] A major survey of the elderly living at home found that of those elderly people with living relatives, over 50% received a visit at least once a week, and almost a third 'several times' a week.[10]

Table 13. Elderly people in private households: by type of household Great Britain, 1978-1979

	Men				Women				All aged 65+
	65-74	75-84	85+	All 65+	65-74	75-84	85+	All 65+	
Household type (percentages):									
With spouse and others	14	9	6	13	6	3	1	5	8
no others	65	53	28	61	41	18	7	31	43
Total with spouse	80	62	34	73	47	21	8	36	51
Without spouse but with others:									
own children	2	5	18	4	6	10	20	8	6
children-in-law	–	2	9	1	1	5	9	3	2
siblings	2	1	1	2	3	5	3	4	3
other relatives	1	1	2	1	1	2	4	2	2
non-relatives	1	2	3	1	2	2	3	2	2
Total without spouse but with others	7	11	34	9	14	24	39	19	15
Living alone	14	27	32	18	39	55	53	45	34
Total in private households	100	100	100	100	100	100	100	100	100

Source: **Social Trends** 11, Table 3.12

However, at the other extreme, as Table 14 shows, 5% never received a visit, and this rose to a worrying 8% for the bedfast and housebound, a higher proportion of whom had no living relatives outside the household. Not surprisingly, single people are less likely to receive visits than those who are married or widowed, but it is also noticeable that the divorced or separated are less likely to receive visits. Only 16% of this group received visits 'several times a week', and almost 13% never did so. Nonetheless over a quarter of elderly people would like to have more visits from relatives — and this is particularly true of the very old, the single, and divorced people.[11] More old people receive visits from relatives than from friends, but those who had fewer visits from relatives received correspondingly more from friends.[12]

The most frequent visitors to elderly people are their children or children-in-law and it is to the family that many elderly people turn for help.[13] At the same time many elderly people are themselves a source of help and support for their families: over a third of elderly people visit their relatives once a week or more frequently, and about a fifth say that they 'are able to do things to help' when they visit.[14] And other forms of contact, telephone calls and letters, are also important. Overall, then, apart from a minority of the elderly, family networks are an important part of their daily lives. There is cause for concern, however, about those who are socially isolated. Moreover, elderly people who were born overseas, and are separated from their families may be particularly at risk.[15]

Table 14. Frequency of visits from relatives (by marital status, mobility and size of household) England, 1976

	Total	Marital status				Mobility		Persons in household		
		Married	Widowed	Single	Divorced	B'fast, house bound	Goes out	One	Two	Three
All elderly persons WEIGHTED	(3,869)	(2,029)	(1,451)	(304)	(85)	(174)	(3,695)	(1,144)	(2,120)	(605)
(unweighted figures)	(2,622)	(1,297)	(1,069)	(208)	(48)	(150)	(2,472)	(809)	(1,406)	(407)
	%	%	%	%	%	%	%	%	%	%
Frequency of visits:										
Several times a week	32.9	33.3	37.4	13.8	16.5	25.9	33.3	39.0	32.3	23.8
At least once a week	21.5	24.0	20.1	12.5	15.3	24.7	21.3	19.3	22.9	20.3
About once a fortnight	6.8	7.6	6.4	3.6	3.5	5.2	6.8	5.9	7.4	6.1
About once a month	8.6	9.5	8.1	6.6	3.5	3.4	8.9	7.1	9.7	7.8
Less often	19.9	18.5	18.3	34.5	25.9	19.5	19.9	18.1	19.1	26.1
Never	5.0	3.4	4.6	16.4	12.9	8.0	4.9	6.4	4.2	5.8
No living relatives outside household	5.3	3.6	5.1	12.5	22.4	13.2	4.9	4.2	4.5	10.1
Total	100.0	100.0	100.0	100.0	100.0	100.0	100.0	100.0	100.0	100.0

Source: A Hunt, **The Elderly at Home**, Table 12.8.1.

Part 9

Family trends and social policy: continuity and change

This final chapter starts by summarising the evidence about family patterns and considers questions of continuity and change. It concludes by noting some of the policy implications of the trends described in the paper.

Table 15. Households: by type Great Britain

	%					
	1961	1966	1971	1976	1978	1979
No family:						
one person —						
under retirement age	4	5	6	6	7	8
over retirement age	7	10	12	15	15	15
two or more people —						
one or more over						
retirement age	3	3	2	2	2	2
all under retirement age	2	2	2	1	1	1
One family:						
married couple only	26	26	27	27	27	27
married couple with 1 or 2						
dependent children	30	27	26	26	26	25
married couple with 3 or						
more dependent children	8	9	9	8	7	6
married couple with independent child(ren) only	10	10	8	7	7	7
lone parent with at least one dependent child	2	2	3	4	4	4
lone parent with independent child(ren) only	4	4	4	4	3	4
Two or more families	3	2	1	1	1	1
Total households	100	100	100	100	100	100

Source: **Social Trends** 11, Table 2.2

There have been, and continue to be, important changes in family patterns. A model of the typical family as 'a nuclear family unit comprising the two natural parents and their respective legitimate child or children living together in their own homes' is, in some senses, increasingly unrealistic.[1] As Table 15 shows married couple families with dependent children living with them make up only about one third of **households** at any one time — and only about 40% if independent children are included. If the stereotype is drawn even more tightly — with mother at home and father as 'breadwinner' — then this would apply to only about 15% of households.[2] And if only 'natural' parents were included, it would be a smaller proportion still. Increasing divorce and remarriage, the rising numbers of one parent families, more dual worker families, and the different patterns among ethnic minority groups are changing the meaning of 'family' for a substantial minority of parents and children. And for some children, family life may be interrupted by periods in residential care or may be in foster or adoptive families.

Yet there is a need for a balanced view of these changes; such a snapshot picture of household composition tends to exaggerate the diversity of family situations.

Chart 11. People in households: by type of household and family
Great Britain, 1979

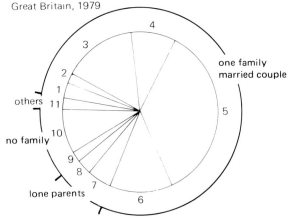

1 No children, wife aged 16-29 3%

2 No children, wife aged 30-44 2%

3 No children, wife aged 45 & over 16%

4 Independent children only 9%

5 One or two dependent children 36%

6 Three or more dependent children 13%

7 Lone parent family, one or more dependent children 5%

8 Lone parent, all children independent 3%

9 Two or more people 2%

10 One person 9%

11 More than one family 2%

Source: **Social Trends 11**, Chart 2.1

The distinction between **households** and **families** made here, is an important one. Households are groups of people who live and eat together, while families are normally defined as a married couple with or without children, or a lone parent with children. We may (or may not) belong to families, but we all live in households, and one of the most significant social trends of this century has been the emergence of increasing numbers of 'no family' households. Trends since 1961 are shown in Table 15, and the 1979 picture in Chart 11. Young people have been increasingly able to move out of the family home before marriage, and increasing numbers of older people are able to maintain independent households. But, as we have shown, many elderly people remain part of an 'extended' family.

Equally important is that such a snapshot picture encapsulates a number of stages in the life cycle. Families currently without dependent children may have had such children in the past, or may do so in the future. Thus, while only 40% of families contain children at one point in time, over 80% will do so at some stage in the life cycle. And looked at from the point of children, the majority are still brought up in a married couple family where both parents are their natural parents. On the other hand, a snapshot, cross sectional picture understates, as we have noted previously, the number of parents and children who will pass through a one parent stage. Similarly the diversity implied by reconstituted, adoptive and foster families is not evident from a cross sectional picture and the diversity of family situations **within** these groups is also important.

The other major move away from a stereotyped model family is the dual worker household, and there is no doubt that the employment of women, and particularly mothers, outside the home is one of the most significant social changes affecting family life. But does the increased employment of women negate the traditional family model described at the beginning of this section? In 1979 it was still true that 50% of children under fifteen years of age had a mother doing no paid work, and only 14% of such children had mothers who worked full time.[3] On the other hand, far more mothers will work at some stage during their children's lives, and many will work part time to enable them to combine work and family responsibilities. We need, therefore, to take a longer term perspective. Even though the majority of parents, children and families still follow a fairly traditional pattern, the minority who do not is growing, and this raises substantial policy questions.

63

Implications for public policy

Many of the changes in family patterns described in this report
have important implications for public policy, and it is perhaps
worthwhile to indicate the nature of some of these.

Social planning and demographic change

First there are changes in the numbers found in different age
groups. Although rapid or substantial changes in the **number** of
births in any one year may be a poor guide to changes in
completed family size, they do have implications for the
provision of public services; specifically maternity and
education services. The post war bulges in the number of
children born has meant alternating periods of expansion and
contraction in the maternity services and in schools. A period
of rapid expansion in teacher supply, with inducements to
married women teachers to return to work, and an extension
of the range of post-graduate teaching qualifications, has
been followed by a drastic reduction in teacher training
facilities. Primary schools have, over the last few years,
found themselves facing successively smaller intakes of pupils,
and these changes are now being felt severely in secondary
schools. Soon they will be felt in sixth forms and in higher
education — and the range of curricular provision may be
affected.[4] There is now the prospect that the recent increase
in the number of births, although small in comparison with
the longer term decline, will mean that the contraction will
have to be put into reverse in a few years' time.[5] The idea of
long term planning for services is very complex in the light of
these demographic swings.

While the number of school age children has declined
significantly, at the other end of the life cycle there is an
equally dramatic **increase** in the elderly population: between
1975 and the year 2001 the number of over-seventy-fives will
increase by some three-quarters of a million and most of this
increase is occurring now — in the decade 1976-85.[6] This trend
has important implications for social planning and for public
expenditure: spending on health and personal social services is
seven times higher for a person over seventy-five than for a
person of working age. The provision of retirement pensions is
a substantial and growing part of the social security budget
and an estimated one-third of all expenditure on social
programmes goes on the elderly.[7] The 'ageing' of the
population focusses attention on the caring capacity and role
of the extended family. And the recent White Paper 'Growing
Older' stated that 'Care in the community must increasingly

mean care **by** the community'[8]. 'Community' care very often simply means family care, and 'family' care, in practice, often means **female** care.[9]

Women

Single women who used to bear the main burden of care for elderly parents are now far less numerous, because of the higher rates of marriage that prevailed up to the 1970s. In the future, then, it will be married women who are likely to be caring not only for their children, but for their parents. Indeed it has been estimated that between the ages of thirty-five and sixty-four 1 in 2 'housewives' can expect at some time or another to give help to an elderly or infirm person. The same 1967 survey showed that 1 in 5 housewives between thirty-five and forty-nine years of age currently had a disabled person or someone aged over sixty-five in the household. And this was true of 1 in 4 of those aged between fifty and sixty-four.[10] For some, this caring role may mean sacrificing their own careers and restricting their life styles.[11] This is an often underestimated 'cost' of the emphasis on 'community care'.[12]

For many people a family means parents and dependent children. But increasingly, as we have indicated, public policy will need to focus on children and 'dependent' parents. Increasing divorce is an important factor here and it will become more important in the future. Studies of the elderly have shown that the divorced and separated have fewer ties with their families than others. In one study 77% of the divorced and separated considered that they have 'close relatives' compared with 96% of the married, 95% of those who were widowed and 87% of those who were single.[13] The changing role of women and the impact of this on the family has a number of public policy implications. We have shown that changes in women's fertility and child bearing patterns have been related to changes in their employment behaviour. Women are now more likely than previously to work between marriage and the birth of their first child, and to rejoin the labour force shortly after completing their families.

Many more women, then, are combining the roles of mother and worker, and this has important implications for the organisation of employment opportunities. Another important policy question concerns child care facilities. In other countries, where the participation of women in the labour market is in general lower than that in Britain, the current debate concerns how far services for working mothers and their children should be extended, and in what form. In Britain, in contrast, there is still a very real debate about the desirability or otherwise of extending child care facilities, if in consequence more mothers were able to return to employment. People disagree about whether the best place for the young child is with its mother, and about the respective rights of mothers to work and of children to be cared for full time by their mothers. But the consequence of this dilemma is that the level of child care facilities provided is well below that which is desired by parents, and means that many parents — and the burden usually falls on the mother — have to make complex arrangements for the care of their children while they are at work.[14] Many mothers work out of economic necessity, and were it not for their earnings some three or four times as many families would be in poverty.[15]

The increased employment of women also has implications for the tax system which is still heavily based on traditional assumptions about the role of men and women within the family. A recent Green Paper is the latest in a number of documents which discuss this complex subject.[16] Much of our social security system is also based on notions of the dependency of women on their husbands which were enshrined in the Beveridge report. Women, on marriage, he argued, acquired a right to support from their husbands, and would turn to them as their first line of support. The national insurance and supplementary benefits systems therefore give a special — and some would argue discriminatory — position to the married woman.[17]

Children

A significant minority of children can expect to experience separation from one or other of their natural parents, and in some cases from their brothers and sisters. A number of others will have new parent figures and new siblings. Smaller families, working mothers and having grandparents alive for much of their childhood are all part of contemporary family life for children. Children in ethnic minority groups — some 90% of whom were born in Britain[18] — may face particular difficulties in reconciling parental values and traditions with those of their peers.

Divorce and one parent families

Much of this paper has been concerned with the state of marriage in Britain: it has described the increasing levels of divorce and remarriage and the growing number of one parent families. Social policy is taking a long time to come to terms with these trends. Some would place emphasis on the **prevention** of marital breakdown[19] but, at least for the foreseeable future, more couples will divorce and the one parent families so formed face a bewilderingly complex and fragmented 'system' of income support. There is much current debate about the obligation of spouses to maintain each other after divorce, and whether existing law in this field should be changed.[20] Where children are involved the issue is different to that of the case of a childless couple. But there is a very real problem that a majority of men's wages are inadequate to support two families — yet with increasing remarriage this situation is likely to become more and more common. People hold very sincere and contradictory views about the way in which public policies should deal with marriage breakdown. The symbolic role of law and public policy in reinforcing or undermining the idea of marriage as an institution should not be underestimated.

Similar issues arise with the way in which cohabitation is treated. Often, in the field of private law a cohabitee is treated as a wife or husband. But in much social security and tax law, cohabitation in some cases 'disenfranchises' women in the same way as if they were married but in others it fails to give them the rights to benefits to which they would be entitled were they in fact married.[21] Closely related to this issue is the legal status of illegitimate children, which has been investigated by the Law Commission.[22]

A family perspective in policy-making

The above discussion illustrates the range of policy issues that are affected by changing family patterns. The Study Commission on the Family is exploring the policy implications of current and future family trends and this requires specific and detailed studies in a number of areas. However, one general point should be emphasised. Whether or not Britain requires an overall 'family policy', it certainly needs to develop a family 'perspective' in policy-making. Such a perspective requires a careful monitoring of demographic trends and a critical evaluation of current policies — and future policy proposals — in the light of changing family patterns. Governments, voluntary organisations, employers and trade unions need to be more aware of the ways in which family patterns are changing. Legislation and policy sometimes assumes a model British family which does not match reality, and is insensitive to the implications of current trends.

A family perspective in policy making would also be based on a sounder understanding of family functions and roles. In areas such as the care of children and the elderly, health and education, we need a more effective 'partnership' between the family and the state. For this to be more than rhetoric we need a closer knowledge of what families are capable of, and willing to do, and what complex of services and benefits they require.

The third dimension to a family perspective is the evaluation of the impact of policies on families. Here, the idea of 'family impact statements' may be useful, and again, it is important to build into the policy making process more effective monitoring and evaluation. We hope this paper will contribute to the development of such a family perspective.

Methodological issues and definitions

There are two major types of problems in interpreting the statistical data on families. First the 'internal validity' or the reliability of the statistics — whether they measure the same thing over time, and measure what they purport to measure. Secondly, the 'external validity' of the statistics — that is whether they are relevant to the particular concepts in which we are interested — how far is divorce, for example, a valid indicator of marriage breakdown? In addition there are often delays in publishing statistics — which means that the question 'what is the situation now?' may be difficult to answer.

The last comprehensive count of families, for example, was the 1971 Census of Population, and comparable data from the 1981 Census will not be readily available until 1983-84. This is a minor problem however compared with predicting what will happen in the future (a problem often overcome by showing a number of variant projections) or with trying to **interpret** the apparent changes in behaviour. Here there is often confusion between the two major types of data available: period and cohort indicators.

Period (or cross-sectional) indicators refer to a situation 'at one point in time' whereas cohort (or longitudinal data) refers to the experience of a group (or cohort) over time. Cohort analysis is probably the most valuable way of identifying changes in behavioural patterns, but there are a number of drawbacks. Firstly, comprehensive longitudinal data is only now being developed and exploited, and current knowledge still relies heavily on the sample survey. Such surveys are often costly, and may not therefore be replicated sufficiently frequently for a long term picture to be built up. Secondly, there is a fundamental problem of the time period involved. For example, if the majority of children are born within ten years of marriage, we need to wait ten years before we can adequately comment on the behaviour of a particular marriage cohort. Thirdly, and perhaps most importantly, we need to decide which cohort base to use; yet in doing so we may be making unwarranted assumptions about causal relationships. What, for example, determines a woman's fertility pattern? — her year of birth (in which case birth cohorts should be used), her year of marriage (in which case her marriage cohort should be used), or even whether there are a large number of other women producing children at the same time — a type of communal psychology? And of course we should recognise men's influence on women's fertility behaviour as well. A good example here is 'what is average family size?'. In 1979, the General Household Survey (GHS) shows that there were on average 1.9 **dependent** children in a married couple family. However, such families include those who also have independent children (and whose actual family size is therefore larger) and families who have not completed their family building (and are thus smaller than their eventual family size). The timing of births can therefore affect our view of family size, and there have been some important changes in the timing of births — especially first births — in recent years. Demographers therefore tend to talk about 'Total Period Fertility Rates'.

In 1979 the Total Period Fertility Rate (TPFR) was between 1.8 and 1.9, having fallen from 2.4 in 1971. Complicating factors are the increasing number of one parent families — whose family size is on average smaller than that of two parent families — and the growing number of 'reconstituted families' produced by remarriage, in which the fertility behaviour of women is not yet adequately documented. Similar problems arise in trying to determine whether 'marriage has become less popular' and is being 'replaced' by cohabitation.

A further problem is to distinguish between demographic 'stocks' and 'flows'. At any one time the population will be composed of various numbers of individuals who are single, married, divorced, cohabiting, childless, etc. Over time, each group will be joined by others, and some of the group will leave. Thus both the **size** and **composition** of a group may change over time, according to the level of flows into and out of the group. (This type of analysis is discussed in the section on single parent families.) However, not all such movements are 'caught' by official statistics, the majority of which are derived from administrative procedures, and information from small scale surveys is particularly useful in this situation.

Family and Household

The main focus of the paper is on families, and the terms 'family' and 'household' have distinct meanings. Households are groups of people who live and eat together, while families are defined as married couples (with or without children) or lone parents with children. An increasing number of household are 'no family' households — 26% in 1979 — but this does not mean that the individuals in these households do not belong to families, or have no contact with their families. Households may increasingly be 'nuclear' but kin and friendship networks are important aspects of family patterns.

Methodological problems in computing the number of one-parent families

The original Finer Report estimates were derived from the 1971 Census — a 1% sample. This methodology was unsatisfactory for identifying some unmarried mothers who were living with their parents. If an unmarried mother lived in a household headed by her own parent(s) both she and her child(ren) were treated as children within a family headed by her father or mother, and thus the probable number of unmarried mothers was understated. For the 1981 Census new procedures are being devised to more adequately pick out these cases. Similarly, although the Census can identify married women with children but no usually resident spouse, it cannot distinguish between temporary and permanent separation of a spouse. On the other hand the General Household Survey does include a 'separated' category and most married lone mothers describe themselves in this way. It also contains a 'married' lone mother category and it should be noted that such lone married mothers may have husbands who usually work away from home or are usually absent for some reason other than the breakdown of the marriage. It has been estimated that about two-thirds of lone married mothers identified in the GHS are in this position.

The other major concern with data from the 1971 Census was in identifying cohabitation. The Census defined a family as either 'a married couple with or without their never-married child or children' or 'a mother or father together with her or his never-married children'. Any additional individual who is normally resident in a household but who could not be allocated to a family unit on this basis was described as 'a household member not in the family'. This led some unmarried couples living together as husband and wife to be identified as separate units — either as two lone parents if they both had children, or as a lone parent plus an unrelated person living in the same household. Although economic necessity often prompts lone parents to share a household — and an estimate from the 1971 Census suggested that 28% of lone parents were living with other persons — obviously a proportion of this group will be living in de facto unions. Of the 139,000 households identified as 'lone-parents and children and others' about 100,000 lived in households containing unrelated adults of both sexes. Of these, an analysis of the GHS suggests that only about half are in fact cohabiting.

A further refinement related to the ratios of motherless to fatherless families identified by the Census and the GHS. In the GHS the ratio of motherless to fatherless families for the period 1971-77 was 1:7. The Census and Finer Ratios were 1:4.5 and 1:5.2 respectively, suggesting an overstatement of the number of motherless families in the latter. In the absence of the 1976 Census, and until the results from the 1981 Census are available, official estimates of one-parent families have derived from a combination of the GHS and the Census. There are in addition estimates, particularly on family size, available from the administration of child benefits. supplementary benefits, widows' benefit and so on. This method uses the fact that where there is only one parent, only one name appears on the order book, and the National Council for One Parent Families is convinced that this method is as accurate as any other existing means for counting one parent families, and provides the most comprehensive and up-to-date information available.

References

Abbreviations

ABAFA   Association of British
Adoption & Fostering
Agencies (now 'BAAF'
– British Association of
Adoption & Fostering)

CPRS   Central Policy Review
Staff

CSO   Central Statistical
Office

DHSS   Department of Health
and Social Security

GHS   General Household
Survey

HMSO   Her Majesty's
Stationery Office,
London

MRC   Medical Research
Council

OPCS   Office of Population
Censuses and Surveys

1 The wider context

1
Government Actuary's
Department (1980) **Population
Projections 1978-2018,** OPCS,
HMSO, Table Appendix IV.C.
2
ibid
3
OPCS (1978) **Demographic
Review 1977,** HMSO, p.3.
4
CSO (1980) **Social Trends 11,**
HMSO, Table 3.10 and p.47.
5
DHSS (1981) **Growing Older**
Cmnd 8173, HMSO.
6
Immigrant Statistics Unit (1977)
'New Commonwealth and
Pakistani Population Estimates',
Population Trends 9, HMSO, p.6.
7
F Glendenning (ed) (1979) **The
Elders in Ethnic Minorities,**
Commission for Racial Equality,
London.

8
OPCS (1980) (a) **Birth Statistics
1978,** HMSO, Table 1.1b, p.16.
9
R M Finer (1974) **Report of the
Committee on One Parent
Families,** Vol I, Cmnd 5629,
HMSO, p.23.
10
Immigrant Statistics Unit (1978)
'Marriage and Birth Patterns
among the New Commonwealth
and Pakistani Populations',
Population Trends 11, HMSO, p.8.
11
OPCS (1978) op cit, p.12,
para 1.9.
12
OPCS ibid, *and* OPCS (1980)
(b) **Marriage and Divorce
Statistics 1978,** FM2, no 5,
HMSO, Table 1.1b; data refers to
England and Wales.

2 Marriage

1
R Leete (1979) **Changing Patterns
of Family Formation and
Dissolution in England and Wales
1964-1976,** OPCS, HMSO, p.20.
2
OPCS (1978) op cit, p.52.
3
OPCS (1981) (c) **Population
Trends 22,** HMSO, p.6.
4
R M Finer (1974) Op cit,
para 2.4, p.6.
5
K Dunnell (1979) **Family
Formation 1976,** OPCS, HMSO,
Table 2.6, p.8.
6
OPCS (1981) op cit, p.2.
7
K Dunnell (1979) op cit, p.5.
8
R Leete (1979) op cit, p.22.

9
K Dunnell (1979) op cit, p.7.
10
ibid, p.5.
11
R Leete (1979) op cit, p.15.
12
K Dunnell (1979) op cit, p.14.
13
ibid, p.18.

3 Fertility and patterns of childbearing

1
C Carter, J Ermish and F Ruffett (1979) Swings for the Schools, Policy Studies Institute, London, and CPRS (1977) Population and the Social Services, HMSO.
2
M Britton (1980) 'Recent Trends in Births', Population Trends 20, OPCS, HMSO, p.4.
3
A H Halsey (1978) Change in British Society, Oxford University Press, Oxford, p.96.
4
OPCS (1978) op cit, p.16.
5
CSO (1980) op cit, Table 2.6, p.30; this is cross-sectional data.
6
K Dunnell (1979) op cit, p.86.
7
CSO (1980) op cit, Table 3.2, p.42.
8
K Dunnell (1979) op cit, Table 4.8.
9
OPCS (1981) Monitor FMI 81/I; figures refer to England and Wales.
10
CSO (1980) op cit, Table 3.17, p.50.
11
ibid, Table 2.16; these figures refer to England and Wales.
12
OPCS (1980) (c) op cit, p.3.
13
The Law Commission (1979) Family Law: Illegitimacy Working Paper 74, HMSO.
14
M Britton (1980) op cit; this is based on experience in Scotland where different birth registration data are collected.
15
OPCS (1980) (c) op cit, p.3.
16
OPCS (1981) Birth Statistics 1979, HMSO, p.36.
17
K Kiernan (1980) 'Patterns of Family Formation and Dissolution', paper given at the Conference on the Implications of Current Demographic Trends in the UK for Social and Economic Policy, York 1980, OPCS, p.27.
18
CSO (1980) op cit, pp.35 and 36.
19
ibid, p.35.
20
ibid, p.36.
21
K Dunnell (1979) op cit, Table 4.3.
22
OPCS (1980) (a) op cit, Table 9.4.
23
K Dunnell (1979) op cit, p.69.
24
ibid, p.86.
25
ibid, p.73.
26
ibid, p.79.

4 Marriage breakdown and divorce

1
OPCS (1978) op cit, p.59.
2
OPCS (1980) (b) Table 4.3; there is an important distinction between the de facto and de jure durations of marriage which is not reflected in these statistics.
3
OPCS (1979) Population Trends 19, HMSO, p.4.
4
OPCS (1978) op cit, p.61. and R Leete and S Anthony (1979) 'Divorce and Remarriage: a record linkage study', Population Trends 16, OPCS, HMSO.

5
K Dunnell (1979) op cit, p.36.
6
ibid, Table 7.2, p.35.
7
ibid, p.36.
8
ibid, p.37.
9
ibid, p.38.
10
B Thornes and D Collard (1979) **Who Divorces?** Routledge and Kegan Paul, London.
11
ibid, p.32.
12
OPCS (1980) (b), Table 4.5. *and* CSO (1980) op cit, Table 2.14.
13
OPCS (1980) **Monitor FM2 80/I.**
14
R Leete (1979) op cit, p.101.
15
ibid, p.103.

5 One-parent families

1
R M Finer (1974) op cit.
2
National Council for One Parent Families (1980) **Annual Report 1979-80,** The Council, London, p.14
3
Community Relations Commission (1978), **Evidence to the Royal Commission on the Distribution of Income and Wealth,** selected evidence for Report no.6, Lower Incomes, HMSO, p.94.
4
R Lister (nd) **As man and wife?** A study of the cohabitation rule, Poverty Research Series no.2, Child Poverty Action Group, London.
5
R Leete (1978), 'One Parent Families: Numbers and Characteristics', **Population Trends 13,** OPCS; HMSO, p.6.
6
R Lister (nd) op cit.
7
OPCS (1980) **Monitor GHS 80/I,** OPCS, Table 3.
8
B Jackson, (1981) 'Single Parent Families' in R N Rapoport, M P Fogarty and R Rapoport (eds), **Families in Britain: Yesterday, Today and Tomorrow,** Routledge and Kegan Paul, London.
9
OPCS (1980) **General Household Survey 1978,** HMSO, Table 2.23.
10
ibid, Table 2.22.
11
ibid, Table 2.24.
12
P Glick (1979) 'Children of Divorced Parents in Demographic Perspective', **Journal of Social Issues,** Vol 35 no.4.
13
R Davie, N Butler and H Goldstein (1972) **From Birth to Seven,** Longman in association with the National Children's Bureau, p.40.
L Lambert and J Streather (1980) **Children in Changing Families,** Macmillan/National Children's Bureau, London, p.56.
E Ferri (1976) **Growing up in a one parent family,** National Foundation for Educational Research, Windsor, p.36.
L Lambert (1978) Living in one parent families: school leavers and their future, **Concern,** National Children's Bureau, no.29, p.26.
14
L Lambert (1978) op cit, p.26.
15
I Burnell and J Wadsworth (1981) Personal communication from the Child Health and Education Study, University of Bristol.
16
ibid.
17
L Lambert and J Streather (1980) op cit, p.57.
18
R Filinson (1981) 'Illegitimacy as Deviance' (unpublished paper) MRC Medical Sociology Unit, Aberdeen, p.14.

19
E Ferri (1976) op cit, p.37.
20
I Burnell and J Wadsworth (1981), op cit.
21
L Lambert (1978) op cit, p.26.
22
National Council for One Parent Families (1980) op cit, Table 4, p.25.

6 Remarriage

1
OPCS (1979) Population Trends 18 HMSO, p.4.
2
OPCS (1980) (b) op cit, Table 3.7.
3
R Leete (1979) op cit p.44.
4
R Leete and S Anthony (1979) op cit p.8.
5
M Britton (1980) op cit p.6.
6
J Burgoyne and D Clark (1980) 'Why get married again?', New Society, Vol. 52, no.913.
7
This is currently being researched by David Clark at the MRC Aberdeen.
8
M Britton (1980) op cit, p.6.
9
J Burgoyne and D Clark (1981), paper given at the Eugenics Society.
10
OPCS (1981) Monitor FM2 81/I.
11
OPCS (1979) Marriage and Divorce Statistics 1976, HMSO, Table 4.6. and OPCS (1981) Monitor FM2 81/2.

7 Reconstituted or blended families

1
E Ferri (1976) op cit, p.34.
L Lambert and J Streather (1980) op cit, p.56.

L Lambert (1978) op cit, p.26.
R Davie, N Butler and H Goldstein (1972) op cit, p.40.
2
E Ferri (1976) op cit, p.33, quoting JWB Douglas (1970) 'Broken families and child behaviour', Journal of the Royal College of Physicians, 4.3, pp.203-10.
3
I Burnell and J Wadsworth (1981) op cit.
4
E Ferri (1976) op cit, p.34.
5
K Fogelman (1976) Britain's Sixteen Year Olds, National Children's Bureau, London, Table 7.1.
6
R Leete (1978) 'Trends in Adoption 1951-1977', Population Trends 14, OPCS, HMSO.
7
The Law Commission (1979) op cit, p.20.
8
R Parker (1978) 'Foster Care in Context', Adoption and Fostering 93, ABAFA, London.

8 Old age and the extended family

1
DHSS (1981) op cit.
2
E Shanas, P Townsend et al (1968) Old People in Three Industrial Societies, Routledge and Kegan Paul, London, Table VI.6.
3
M Abrams (1980) Beyond Three Score Years and Ten, A second report on a survey of the Elderly, Age Concern, London, p.8. and CPRS and CSO (1980) People and their Families, HMSO, para 5.2.3.
4
DHSS (1981) op cit, para 6.2.
5
CSO (1980) op cit, Table 2.2.
6
ibid, chart 3.12.

7
OPCS (1973) **General Household Survey: Introductory Report,** HMSO, p.55.

8
CPRS (1980) op cit, para 5.3.1.

9
A Hunt (1978) **The Elderly at Home: A study of people aged sixty-five and over living in the community in England in 1976,** HMSO, Table 12.3.1.

10
ibid, Table 12.8.1.

11
ibid, p.97.

12
ibid, p.98.

13
ibid, Table 12.11.1.

14
ibid, p.101.

15
DHSS (1981) op cit, para 6.6.

9 Family trends and social policy: continuity and change

1
R Rapoport, R N Rapoport and Z Strelitz (1977) **Fathers, Mothers and Others,** Routledge and Kegan Paul, London, p.88.

2
OPCS (1980) **Monitor, GHS 80/I** shows that 52% of women with dependent children were economically active in 1979.

3
CSO (1980) op cit, Table 3.2.

4
E Briault and F Smith (1980) **Falling Rolls in Secondary Schools,** NFER Publishing Company, Windsor.

5
See C Carter, J Ermish and F Ruffett (1979) op cit.

6
DHSS/Welsh Office (1978) **A Happier Old Age,** HMSO, para 1.1.

7
ibid, para 1.9.

8
DHSS (1981) op cit, para 1.9.

9
J Finch and D Groves (1980) 'Community Care and the Family: A case for Equal Opportunities?' **Journal of Social Policy,** Vol 9 part 4.

10
A Hunt (1970) **The Home Help Service in England and Wales,** HMSO, p.424, quoted in H Land (1978) 'Who Cares for the Family', **Journal of Social Policy,** Vol 7 part 3 p.360.

11
Equal Opportunities Commission (1980) **The Experience of Caring for Elderly and Handicapped Dependants: survey report,** EOC, Manchester.

12
DHSS (1981) **Care in Action,** HMSO, Appendix 2, p.47.

13
A Hunt (1978) op cit, p.94.

14
See for example, B Bryant, M Harris and D Newton (1980) **Children and Minders,** Grant McIntyre, London.

15
L Hamill (1978) **Wives as Sole and Joint Breadwinners,** Government Economic Service Working Paper no.15, DHSS, London, p.13.

16
The Taxation of Husband and Wife (1980), Cmnd 8093, HMSO.

17
H Land (1978) op cit.

18
CPRS (1980) op cit.

19
See for example Home Office/DHSS (1979) **Marriage Matters,** HMSO. **and** J Dominian (1980) **Marriage in Britain 1945-1980,** Study Commission on the Family, London.

20
The Law Commission (1980) **The Financial Consequences of Divorce: the Basic Policy,** Cmnd 8041, HMSO.

21
D Pearl (1979) 'Cohabitation in England: Social Security and

Supplementary Benefits
Legislation', **Family Law,** Vol.9
no.8.
22
The Law Commission (1979)
op cit.